THE MAKING OF LOVE

HOW TO STAY IN LOVE AS A COUPLE
THROUGH THICK & THIN (EVEN WITH KIDS!)

STEVE & SHAARON BIDDULPH

Illustrations by John Wright

DOUBLEDAY

Sydney   Auckland   New York   Toronto   London

Acknowledgements

Especial thanks to Ken and Elizabeth Mellor, whose mastery of both western psychotherapy, and the eastern Vedic tradition, has been a major source for this book, and for our own living and teaching. We have never met kinder, or more potent, teachers.

Thanks to our friends and families, which these days are one and the same.

To transactional analysis' 'grandfather' Robin Maslen for the four Cs of couple communication; and bioenergeticist Julie Henderson, for first teaching us about the nature of contact and attraction.

We're indebted to all those who contributed their personal stories, lending depth and heart to these pages.

For encouragement, to Maggie Vickers, Pat McKenzie and Rob and Miranda Dalton.

Finally to Rex Finch, editor and navigator on corporate seas, who asked for the very book we had in mind to write, so we knew it was meant to be.

THE MAKING OF LOVE
A DOUBLEDAY BOOK
First published in Australia by Doubleday
Reprinted 1992, 1993, 1994, 1995 and 1996 (twice)
© Text, Steve Biddulph and Shaaron Biddulph 1988
© Illustrations, John Wright 1988

National Library of Australia
Cataloguing-in-Publication Entry.

Biddulph, Steve
    The Making of Love: How to stay in love as a
    couple through thick and thin (even with kids).
    Bibliography.
    Includes index.
    ISBN 0 86824 480 5 (cased edition)
    ISBN 0 86824 377 9 (paperback edition)
    1. Interpersonal relations. 2. Parenthood
    I. Biddulph Shaaron, II. Title.
158'.2

Doubleday books are published by
Transworld Publishers (Aust.) Pty Limited
15–25 Helles Avenue, Moorebank, NSW 2170
Transworld Publishers (NZ) Limited
3 William Pickering Drive, Albany, Auckland
Transworld Publishers (UK) Limited
61–63 Uxbridge Road, Ealing London W5 5SA
Bantam Doubleday Dell Publishing Group Inc.
1540 Broadway, New York, New York 10036
Cover design by Lee Marquette
Text designed by Deborah Brash
Typeset by Midland Typesetters, Maryborough, Victoria
Printed by Brown Prior Anderson

It doesn't much matter whether you are the prime minister, or you work in the corner shop . . .

If you win in your lifetime great fame, or great fortune, that's nice, but it doesn't, in the end count for much . . .

You are here, on this planet, to learn to love,

and that's all.

You have always known this.

Contents

CHAPTER 1

We're in This Together

This is a book about liberating yourself through being a partner, and being a parent. It is not just about how to 'cope' with these 'roles' (shudder!) but shows you how to find, in these central parts of your life, joy and fulfilment in abundance.

A book is just someone talking — a rather one sided conversation. Whenever you read a book, or look at a painting or even read graffiti on a wall, you can't help wondering 'Who is the person behind this?'. As you're starting to read this book right now, part of your mind is already trying to form a picture of who we, Steve and Shaaron, are, and what we are like.

About Us

We are very normal. We live in an old wooden house, we laugh a lot, and yell a lot too. We watch 'Sale of the Century', and 'Magnum'. (We used to watch 'Perfect Match' too, but everyone has limits!) We have been together for fifteen years, and have a baby son. We still sometimes get totally confused about communication, but not as often as we once did!

Steve trained as a counselling psychologist, and Shaaron as both a nurse and a social worker. These professions, along with others like psychiatrist, marriage counsellor, even family doctor, have on the surface separate skills, but these days fill an increasingly similar role — of simply being someone to talk to. In our separate jobs we talked to very many people about the problems of living. Steve specialised in family therapy. Shaaron worked with deaf children and adults, and as a nurse tackled especially the emotional side of illness and bereavement.

At the same time as holding these 'responsible' positions, we were ourselves just another young couple starting out in adult life. We spent as much time working out our own lives as being involved in those of other people. We were shy by nature, rather than humble by choice, and found that people appreciated our honesty in admitting that we were only human. This removed barriers, and made our work a success.

We also discovered that people working constantly amid crisis situations can only go one of two ways: they can either 'burn out', or 'tune in'. The latter seemed preferable. Tuning in meant listening very closely to people, looking carefully at every movement and expression, really wanting to understand life through them. At the same time, not 'needing' to help or change others, or prove anything, meant that the pressure was taken off the situation, so real contact could take place. By getting this close to people we found that we began to know and love them, often more than they knew and loved themselves. This included 'ordinary' people, who were easy to like, but also people who were violent, hurtful and just generally unpleasant! We never met anyone with whom we didn't eventually feel some sense of a bond. For healing to take place, we knew that loving was a necessity. We were relieved to find that over the years, this feeling became a reality.

Crisis work is very absorbing, and we might have disappeared into it forever, but for one thing. We began to realise that something very strange was going on with family life in the late twentieth century. Put yourself in our position. If you were to talk to *hundreds* of young parents, all having almost identical problems with their kids, and if you were to meet *dozens* of intelligent, good hearted people who were having inordinate trouble staying married and getting along, you might begin to suspect that normal people are somehow ill-equipped by society for even the basics of living. You might even begin to feel that being normal in our society means being in a mess. That was certainly how it looked to us.

While working with people to ease their distress and hurt, it's natural to start examining your own life, especially your childhood. Steve grew up in a caring, but rather isolated immigrant family. Shaaron was one of five daughters who, with their parents, had to struggle and work very hard when they were young. Neither of our backgrounds were exceptional, yet both of us came to adult life with a great many inbuilt difficulties. We slowly realised, through reading and reflection, and from talking to our patients, that in the times in which we (and you) grew up, an 'average' childhood often meant great deprivation in certain aspects of emotional health. Paradoxically, at the material level, childhood had never been so rich, secure and diverse.

This paradox is the key to understanding life in our culture in this century. Many people who consider themselves 'normal' adults are in fact markedly stunted in emotional growth, and have basically lost trust in relationships. For a large proportion of those growing up in western countries, perhaps since the start of the industrial revolution, a 'normal' childhood has meant considerable emotional pain, confusion and loneliness. We believe that many (if not most) people today need concerted help to begin growing again towards what human beings truly can be.

For a while these thoughts unsettled us greatly, then it dawned on us that, elsewhere in the world, others would surely have addressed this problem. We began to travel and learn from other practitioners, spending time with, in our view, some of the best healers and teachers in the field of family relationships on the planet. Some of these people are famous, and their names would be known to you. Others were so engrossed in their work that they did not always seem to realise the wider significance of it — like explorers who have such fun in the wilderness they forget to come back! Over the last few years, our role has been to make more widely known the missing keys — both ancient and modern — that simplify and clarify the heart of everyday living. Plenty of people have more wisdom than we do, but we do the best job we can of finding it and passing it on.

We now refuse to define people as patients or treat them as sick. We now work only as teachers, meeting daily with groups of people, helping them to heal old pain, clear up confusion, and laugh their way back to happiness. Over 7000 people have spent a day or more with us, (though now, with a family, and more sense, we prefer to work more deeply with smaller numbers). Through our books like *The Secret of Happy Children*, and this book now in your hands, we hope that a few more people can find the pleasure that life is meant to be.

A book can be an impersonal thing. We prefer to work face

to face. When you are sitting down talking for a time with someone, then it's not hard to begin to love them. We may not know you, the reader, on a human scale and perhaps never will. But we want to convey to you the caring behind this book, just as if you were sitting here with us. We hope that a feeling of connectedness grows as you read on. To feel connected, and to feel special, is every child's — and every person's — birthright. The toddler stepping out into the spring garden knows that the sun shines just for him or her. This book was written just for you.

About You

Now let's talk about you! You're probably right in the midst of it all. One day you woke up, and you weren't a child any more. And now here you are. You've made choices, taken directions in life, and though these can be changed, they cannot be wiped out. You've made sex, made love, made commitments, and most likely made children! You have lines on your face, and 'silver hairs among the gold'. You're up to your neck in the great human adventure called 'family'.

Do you ever ask yourself, 'What am I doing with my life? What am I really on about?'. Sometimes we talk to very old people or to people near to death, and these people can be stunningly blunt and clear about life's priorities. They tend to come to the same sorts of conclusions. You can have great achievements behind you, they will say, make lots of money, the whole world might know your name, but what you think of when your time gets short is going to be 'How did I make out with those close to me? Do my children love me, or even like me? Did my partner or partners love me, and do they still?'. And lastly, the most important of all, 'Do I love (or even like) myself?'. In the end it will be the answers to these questions that will either bring you joy or despair when you lie by yourself in the darkness. Now is the time to do something about them.

4

Who wants to be normal?

Our national track record in family living is not terrific. On average 40 000 people a year in Australia (where we live) take a long look at their marriage and decide to give it away. (And each year, with everlasting optimism, more than the same number either marry or move in together to 'give it a go'.) It is becoming the exception for a child to grow up in a family with its original parents still together. The instability of family life is reflected throughout our culture. A teacher no longer risks asking 'What does your daddy do?'. The child may answer 'Which daddy do you mean?', or 'I don't have one', or 'Ask him. He's over there being parent-help!'

Families must change and grow, and break-ups can be a necessary move, important steps to health for all concerned. But it is such a painful way to learn.

J. WRIGHT

Unhappiness shows up in other ways besides divorce. Our overall suicide rate comes close to equalling the much publicised road toll. (In fact the two greatly overlap.) Tranquillisers are the most widely prescribed drugs throughout the western world. Alcoholism is our most common disease. Half our hospital beds are for psychiatric patients.

Yet there are signs of improvement. The divorce rate is falling, and has done so slightly each year since the mid 1980s. People wait longer to marry now, and to have children — presumably out of healthy caution! Divorced people usually remarry, and more people are married (proportionately) than at any time in our history. (Up until this century as many as one-fifth of all adults remained single, and childless, and perhaps disgustingly happy!)

Are you someone important or just a parent?

Family living has been culturally degraded. We still hear women describe themselves as 'just a housewife', and for many men the term 'breadwinner' has a sense of desperation to it. (Perhaps we could change it to 'cakewinner'?)

In other cultures children (and spouse) are a source of pride, but in the west our most fervent hope as we move our family about in public is just to avoid embarrassment! If your children visit you at work, do you glow with pride or do you wince? To travel with young children on public transport is to be in a state of perpetual apology. (This is the direct opposite to most non Anglo-Saxon countries, where children are a passport to endless interest and compliments.) *In our culture we are not encouraged to be proud of our parenthood or our children.* On the contrary — greatness in our society includes almost by definition the failure or neglect of one's family. The leading cultural or political figure whose family is in tatters has become part of the folklore of the western world. This is not unconnected to the state of the world. We are often led by people who have lost their hearts.

The family as a path to liberation

At this point in your life, when you have chosen to pick up and begin reading this book, you may be proceeding very happily. Or, you may be passing through a phase which you consider less than completely successful. If the latter is the case, it is hardly surprising. We do not have a tradition for making marriage work. The sum total of our forebears' message may have been 'you make your bed and lie in it' which is hardly an introduction to the craft of love. Likewise parenting has in the past been carried out in great isolation. We've been brainwashed into seeing it as ordinary, unimportant, like doing the dishes.

As a consequence of these attitudes, many people find family concerns to be a disheartening part of their lives. The home, rather than a harbour of comfort and stimulation, is a source of dismay. It is the place where they feel least successful. If this is to any degree true of you, then it is time you let yourself off the hook. It is vitally important that you recognise how much you are actually succeeding. Our role in guiding many hundreds of families has made this much clear to us: without discounting the very real confusions and mistakes which may at times overwhelm you, you have actually related, communicated, committed, given and received love, and generally succeeded well beyond your conscious knowledge. One day, this will be evident to you.

We are all pioneers. In the past, family relationships were often simply an appearance one kept up. People did not expect intimacy or authentic communication. Rules and clichés governed most interactions. There were always special people seeking something better than the acting out of social roles, but we are the first generation on a wide scale to expect and seek to be real. Sometimes things have to be dismantled in order to be better put together. The surface confusions of our age mask a deeper trend towards improving our lives. In this century at least, there has been a steady progress towards finding, and giving, fulfilment.

Your own challenges, hesitations, and successes are part of this progress. You can no more fail or go backwards in life than a tree can ungrow. If you feel unhappy or stuck at a particular time, realise that this is because part of you senses and yearns for perfection. Part of you knows it is possible. Be grateful for yearnings, which will actually serve to keep you moving on to something better. Keeping this positive perspective will ensure that you relax, trust yourself more, and so continue to progress.

In most eastern traditions there exists the concept of a path, or way of living one's life, which is chosen from alternative paths available. This is very different from our narrower sense of career, since the choice governs one's whole life, not just one's job, and the goal is to become 'realised' or 'complete' rather than to simply achieve material success. One very advanced system (for guiding one's life choices) has existed in written form, and been in continuous practice, for at least 5000 years. Properly called the Vedic tradition, it is known to us by the more common term of yoga. You may have had favourable contact with yoga, or you may regard it with some suspicion. The physical exercises we associate with yoga are only one facet of a system covering health, science, medicine, astronomy, architecture, leadership, physics and so on, which developed when the western world was still in what is called the Middle Stone Age. Ancient texts called the Vedas listed a range of possible ways to conduct one's life, from which a young person would choose that which best suited his or her situation. The ultimate goal of self-perfection could be achieved through any number of completely separate pathways. As you'd expect, these included physical practices, higher meditation, total devotion to a master, charitable service to mankind; but also 'householding — the raising of children and care of family'. It is important to understand that this was no mere concession to the masses. Fatherhood, motherhood, and sexual love were not just tolerated, they were revered.

This bears repeating. *In the ancient systems of self-liberation, to cultivate a lifelong erotic and companionable relationship, to lovingly and attentively raise children, to earn a living by honourable if humble means, and to prepare food and keep house with art and style, was as highly regarded as any way of life one may choose.*

'Huh!' you're saying! 'Nobody reveres me much!' You may well have come to feel that family life is ordinary. After all, you are just doing the same as everyone else! It's an easy mistake to make, for after all, what's enlightening about rushed meals and sleepless nights? From nappies to teenage parties, it all looks like one big chance to fail! Feminist debate still rages about the value of parenthood: many people are concluding that in the rush for equal opportunity at work, women bought the myth that there was something inferior about homekeeping. The secret is in how things are approached. Family life can be drudgery, but it can also be a path to complete inner freedom.

(Lately there has been a great boom in self-development courses and seminars being marketed to a hungry public. You can save your money! Being a parent will teach you assertiveness. You'll get relaxation training (in the guise of fatigue!). You'll acquire communication skills, aerobic exercise, time management and every other kind of self development you could ask for, in a non-stop twenty-year experiential marathon!)

Parenting is a profession. Marriage is a consummate art. While hardly undemanding, these pathways can also be easier and simpler than you ever dreamed. That's what this book is about.

J. WRIGHT

But I want to do something worthwhile!

What *is* worthwhile? If you live long enough, and have time to reflect, you will notice that any aspect of life can be significant. Some things may seem important, and turn out not to be, while others thought of as trivial turn out to be life-changing. Such things can never be known in advance. A kind but quite casual word at the right time may save another's life. A single thought in a quiet moment, or a chance meeting, can change the direction of your own life. Knowing this possibility, and being receptive to it, can fundamentally change every waking moment.

We all have to set priorities in life, deciding from the myriad choices where our time and effort will go. For your priorities to be successful, though, you must start with those things that are fundamental: food, sleep, exercise, time to reflect, the love of those close to you. The nature of human life is such that, if these are not adequate, everything else one does is ungrounded or, if one continues for long enough down this track, literally, insane.

Steve once went to an evening meeting of a community centre committee. The new staff person hired by the committee ran out to the car park to meet us, and to say what a rough day he'd had, he 'Hadn't even had time to go to the toilet!'. During the meeting, he became increasingly defensive and agitated, and later that night was hospitalised with a psychotic episode. Eventually he rested up and got better. Steve couldn't help thinking though — that guy really should have gone to the toilet!

The root and the flower

Everywhere around you, from public figures to people in your neighbourhood, you will see the catastrophic results that arise when people lose perspective. What does this mean in practice? Right now, as we sit talking and preparing this book, our baby son starts calling to be picked up. Our writing work is engrossing to us. But a baby is a baby, and parenthood is our chosen path right now. We cease writing, and a child's needs are met.

It's tempting to judge the worth of your own lives, and the lives of other people, by the yardstick of external achievement. You are *worthwhile* if you make some 'contribution', say, in sport, finance, government, entertainment or charity. You are *important* if you have spending power. There's a commonplace expression which sums up this approach: We say 'Wouldn't it be nice to "*be* somebody"', the implication being that the great mass of us who choose to be partners, parents, and to quietly do a job, are of little worth. If you're not 'somebody', then you're a nobody.

The paradox and tragedy of public life is that choosing a path of external achievement often means choosing a fatal imbalance in one's life. With boring regularity, we read of famous figures whose personal lives are a tangled mess. (Such stories are so often reported that they must be of some comfort and pleasure to ordinary folk!) It is one of the hazards for young people finding an identity today, that the people who are in the public eye, and held up for emulation, often have no possibility of normal family life, no real relaxation, no trust or friendship that is not distorted by the fact of 'who they are'.

Life has to be balanced. If the basics aren't right, then nothing else can be. We personally find it very difficult to manage children well on days when we're not synchronised as a couple — or to do a good job in the wider world. Have you ever experienced racing from a hassled and off-balance beginning at home, and trying to be instantly calm, gracious and friendly at some appointment or meeting? Or had friends drop in when you're midway into a furious fight? It's erroneous to try and 'balance' personal and family life with work life. One is the root, and the other the flower. Feed the root and you will have the flower. Neglect the root and you will have neither.

If you work outside your home, and your work is somewhat less than satisfying, then we may be preaching to the converted! You may have already decided that home and family are the heart of your life. If your work is stimulating, important, demanding, then it may seduce you for a while, but eventually you will have to notice where your roots are. Whatever your work is, it will be peaceful and loving, and 'go right', only if home (and bed) are sources of renewal and joy. This isn't just dutiful 'maintenance' of family and relationships. We're talking about healthy self-interest here — realising that this level is where all of the pleasure and clarity and balance in your *whole* life will spring from.

So! You've chosen the path called family and sometimes it gets hard. You may not have known that it was a path to total self awakening and bliss. Now as you consider that you're climbing the biggest, most glorious mountain there is, it may make both the struggles and the delights a little clearer to you. Our aim here has been to challenge you, to make contact. You will need to read the whole book to understand what we are saying. All real learning requires taking a chance.

This book follows the sequence of the life of a family. The next chapter looks at *compatibility* — the dynamics of attraction and how to create a bond that is fully what we need. Chapter 3 continues into *deepening contact* — the ways by which dialogue, self-exploration, and even fighting will expand the boundaries of your self and your relationship, so that you feel freer with your partner than you thought it was possible to feel. Chapter 4 looks at the arrival of *children*, and how their development activates changes in you at each step of the way. The chapter on *sex and romance* (an inseparable alliance) is deliberately placed after that about children: these two ingredients often come without conscious effort in courtship, but with a house full of kids they require deliberate cultivation. Chapter 6 is entitled *Advanced Lessons* and provides some ongoing challenges about the place of family in the world, and your own personal way of finding freedom and joy in living.

CHAPTER 2

Compatibility:
The Ways We Connect

She:	*We just never agree about anything . . . kids, money, jobs, where to live, what to do.*
He:	*That's not true!*
She:	*See!*
We: (laughing)	*So how did you two get together?*
He: (sits back and smiles)	*We. . .eell. That's another story!*
We:	*Tell us about that . . .*

Liking, Loving and Lust

The family cycle begins, naturally enough, with 'boy meets girl'. It's the attraction of opposites that sparks the explosion that kicks along the whole wheel of life. But attraction is complex. It has many levels to it, and understanding these levels is vital to a successful and happy love life.

For instance, some couples are (surprisingly to some) first attracted at the mind level — *liking* another person's ideas, finding them funny, interesting, stimulating. Other couples may find that they connect initially from the heart level, finding that warmth, affection, and *loving* feelings arise easily between them. And of course many couples begin with the obvious sexual attraction, a tantalising pleasurable excitement that is pure *lust!* For added complexity, you can lust after someone who only likes you, or love someone who can only lust, and so on. It makes things tricky.

A successfully developing partnership will eventually need to involve all three, although the order of unfolding will vary. In this chapter we'll explore how these three powerful forces work, and how in combination they provide a pathway to unprecedented happiness.

J. WRIGHT

A meeting of minds

Let's begin our discussion on safe ground (!) with the 'head' level. Think about the people you talk to at work, or in the street. The conversations you have with casual acquaintances are very simple — 'Isn't the weather awful?'; 'What do you think about this?'; 'Did you notice that!'; 'You reckon we'll win the cricket?'.

Small talk is often dismissed as being superficial, but it can equally be cheering and relaxing, and can even convey deep caring. The content though, is simple and general: information and comment that could be *from* anyone *to* anyone.

Even as friendships develop and things deepen a little, conversations are still basically the exchange of information. We can go for years without talking about anything else but thoughts and information. If people have interesting enough thoughts, that's not too bad. But in courtship and dating behaviour, words are a powerful magic (giving those of us who were tongue-tied adolescents some initial cause for despair). Jokes, repartee, questions and discussions about everything and anything, proclamations of belief and identity, all meet the necessary function of finding out just who you have got your hands on here. But as every would-be partner knows, the words are not the whole story. Underneath the banter and earnestness are questions of a different dimension. 'Do they *like* me?', and 'Do they *want* to know me better?'

The level of attraction we call *liking* has a simple, uncomplicated quality to it. It's independent of age, or sex. You can like someone from afar, a TV personality or an author, and this can be as far as it goes. Sometimes though, when the need is there, attraction of a second, deeper kind flows in behind the first. *Loving* is powerful, and brings in a whole added complexity. It can be expressed in words, or at least hinted at, but it is hard to capture in this way because it is not about words. The heart aches, it sings, and it soars, but it doesn't talk much!

Loving causes alarm in some people because it is part of a domain that is unfamiliar — the domain of emotion. Such alarm is needless. As we will demonstrate, feelings are simple!

Finding your heart

In the structure of the human mind, thoughts, words, ideas and opinions are like the ripples on the surface. They are but a reflection of the deeper currents of feeling that always run beneath. Our brains are physiologically 'wired' in such a way that for every thought we have, there is an accompanying feeling, a second deeper level of meaning that is never absent. Even in everyday relationships with workmates and friends there is a feeling dimension surging along underneath.

Listen, look, and note your own body reactions, and you will be able to pick up the feeling tones behind your outward words and behaviour. Notice how this feeling tone is present in other people's words and behaviour.

The feeling might be symbolised in what is said: *'The weather's awful'* ('and I'm depressed and lonely but I don't know how to tell you').

Or it may be just below the surface, implied but not spoken: *'Have you heard about the reorganisation at work?'* ('It's scaring me to death').

There may be a request that the person cannot yet make openly: *'I really did well today'* ('and I'm proud and want you to praise me').

Or a straight out denial and cover up of the true feelings: *'I'm fine, how are you?'* ('I'm furious, but you wouldn't care . . . would you?').

J. WRIGHT

The feeling level may be expressed openly, or it may simmer underneath, but it is *always* present. Feelings and needs which are uncommunicated do not go away. In fact it is the opposite: they tend to build up and fester, and especially if we deny them to ourselves, can turn into physical as well as mental pain, and often into actual illness.

In our chronically lonely culture, many people simply have no idea what their feelings are telling them, yet their backs and arms yearn for touch, their heart muscles contract in fear, and below a controlled surface they are swept with emotions needing to be heard and understood. You yourself probably have places in your body that frequently feel sore, or ache a lot, or are prone to infection. Slow down reading for a moment, and notice right now how your body is feeling. Notice also how it changes subtly but distinctly as you give it more attention, even as you are reading along right now. If you stay with your body sensations, and at the same time soften and move a little, your body will direct you how to be more comfortable. Now change your focus. Pay attention specifically to the places in your body where you are feeling good — warm, soft, easy and comfortable. Stay with these pleasant sensations, and allow them to spread. Notice how your thoughts now have also steadied and calmed. Our bodies are constantly responding to our thoughts, and to the world around us. Our thoughts in turn are coloured and driven by our feelings. What we call discomfort is simply a signal that we need to do something (often quite small) to find equilibrium again. These signals will tell us a great deal if we listen.

There are always two steps in relating to a partner at the heart level. The first is acknowledging our feelings to ourselves, and the second is communicating them honestly to our partner. By doing this we begin to synchronise our states of being so that loving can arise. We eventually feel merged, comfortable, and stimulated by the other person's presence, and the inputs they make to our own experience.

Listen in on this conversation between a couple in their thirties, just beginning a relationship, and tentatively beginning to communicate loving:

She: Why haven't you been in touch?
He: I didn't think you wanted to see me!
She: But I thought you knew how much I felt for you.
He: Well . . . you get so critical and cold sometimes.
She: I . . . I just don't like to feel controlled that's all.
He: I don't want to control you.
She: I know you don't, it's just, well, I'm anxious about being too close to a man again, I don't seem to choose men well.

He: Thanks very much!
She: Oh, you know what I mean!

Notice that there is no real logic to the above, at least on the surface, and yet there *is* a progression towards closeness and understanding. Of course, disclosing your feelings doesn't guarantee instant harmony! The first stages of self-disclosure may be highly charged, since anger, fear and sadness can also go along with being in love. But, in the long run, honesty creates safety, harmony and balance between people, if for no other reason than that you now *know* where you stand. With feelings undisclosed, we simply wander in confusion. With increasing honesty, as our feelings interreact, we can begin to absorb and clear up the obstacles to our closeness one by one.

So in a relationship worthy of the name, people find attraction growing from head to head, and also from heart to heart. But there's another level too, so let's go on down to the basement!

The fire down below

Sexual attraction is a lifelong, powerful tide which either adds energy and magnetism to relationships, or constantly sweeps things apart, depending on our skill and awareness in navigating it.

Sex puzzles people — it is rarely understood in its proper biological context. You will often hear sex denigrated as the 'animal' part of our make-up, a Stone Age leftover which disturbs our rational mind. In fact human beings are more dedicatedly and enduringly sexual than any other animal species. The much maligned rabbit has nothing on us! In human beings though, the original purpose of the sex-drive — to motivate reproduction — has been partly diverted to serve an equally important role, that of social connection. Although sex often seems to be a disrupting influence on our social fabric, it is nonetheless the force that creates and holds families and communities together. Obligation and duty wear thin very quickly, they are recent and advanced concepts in history: nature counts on much stronger glues to cement us.

Our biology has ensured that we will not rely on abstract ideas of loyalty and love, but that commitment will be deeply felt, that these feelings will give us more pleasure and reward than any other path in the long run. Let's explore this aspect of sexual bonding in more depth.

Our sexuality is connected to our emotions and our thoughts, and has a magnetic way of drawing people into relationships which can then develop far beyond simply lusty desire. In this way it builds between two people an accumulating reserve of pleasure, security, release and openness. Lifelong pair-bonds are common in the animal world (and so is promiscuity, but few species combine them). The unique nature of human sexuality — the intense female orgasm which only humans seem to experience and the absence of the distinct 'on heat' cycle experienced by other mammals — means that (for reasons we do not yet understand) sex is constantly present in our social lives.

In evolutionary terms, pair-bonding meant that the whole fabric of family and clan was made more secure and trustworthy. People could spend time away hunting, children could be raised in relative safety, because the sexually annealed bond between partner-parents meant that they would yearn for the specific company of that one person, above any other.

This carries a risk though. Putting it in simple terms, if you have sex with someone, you are very likely to fall in love with them. It is not a good idea to get bonded to someone whom your heart and head have huge reservations about. This is why human cultures are careful about adolescent sexuality, and why young people themselves, in spite of what adults believe, are actually very conscious about relinquishing (female or male) virginity. In recent research (even before the arrival of AIDS) a surprising 25 per cent of all young people were still virgins at twenty-one.

When 'the fire down below' connects with mental sparkle up top *and* the glow of emotion from the heart, then all three are charged and magnified. (In Chapter 5 this is explored more fully.) Outside of the primary couple, the combinations can vary. Just as you can have an intellectual discussion with someone, where there is brain but no heart involvement, you can equally well have a genital attraction without heart or head communication. Admit it! Or you can *like* someone who you don't *understand* and certainly wouldn't *want to go to bed with*, but the liking is definitely there. We are complex creatures.

The very first moments of meeting, the starting points of our intimate relationships, are interesting to reflect on. Personally speaking, our own first meeting (the only one we can speak about with authority) was clearly love at first touch! Heart connections followed, and only slowly, quite awkwardly, did we learn to talk to each other.

J.WRIGHT

Compatibility Problems

Why men and women sometimes miss

The bioenergetic therapists, who devised these levels of connection, say that men traditionally have 'closed' hearts (shielded, unresponsive) and 'open' (active, energised) genitals, while women traditionally have 'closed' genitals and 'open' hearts. Minds may be closed, open, or off somewhere else! If you are a man, you may have felt for yourself (perhaps with some alarm) the tangible physical sensations in the front muscles of your heart (Good grief! An emotion!) that sometimes come with falling in love, or with seeing your children asleep, being present at a birth, or saying goodbye to someone forever. If you are a woman, you may have loving feelings as a matter of course, but may recall having been stunned and delighted at the energetic glow and sense of new assurance that comes after the first really good sex in your life. 'Traditional' men need to gain the softening that comes from an open heart, then their life expectancy may one day equal that of women! 'Traditional' women need to gain the power that comes from 'owning' their pelvis, considered in both ancient Yoga and contemporary bioenergetics as the energy source of assertiveness and will.

Levels of attraction are especially important to be aware of when looking for a partner. In our workshops we teach people, especially teenagers, to distinguish these three levels of need and, in handling personal relationships, to be honest with themselves about which is what. We think this is the real sex education, and knowing it will prevent countless problems.

Of course the levels swirl and interact together, and we want them to. Remember being an adolescent, and finally getting up the courage to declare our love to the girl (or boy) of our dreams! Having had some friendliness from them in the past, there seems every reason to hope . . . and so we finally take the plunge and declare our love! To our horror, they look alarmed, and utter those fateful words, 'Oh no, oh dear, I really like you, but I . . .' It's lucky that hope springs eternal, or we'd all be hermits.

The three-way connection of liking, love and lust is clearly central to our make-up. When you do finally find someone that you connect with on all three levels, the total effect is much greater than the separate parts, and meets the two obvious criteria for a good love-match — feelings which are both powerful and enduring.

Sometimes people suggest that love is an illusion, brainwashed into us through pop songs and mushy movies. The evidence is strong, though, that all people, even avowed loners, are aware of the possibility of love. The external cues resonate in tune with a timeless inner signal. We seek total love because we know it to be possible.

It only hurts when you lie

A second problem, which many single people today experience, comes through the attempt to be sexual first, and committed 'later, maybe'.

Society has gone through major shifts in recent decades in its handling of the sex-bonding dynamic. We are living in the aftermath of the 1960s, a period in which many people attempted to define sex as primarily an *experience*, as opposed to a *relationship*. This was part of an important and very beneficial freeing of attitudes, a change of truly historic proportions. (This same generation also rejected the conventional in many other spheres — in dress, diet, ritual, music, life values and goals. They declared [however idealistically], a commitment to personal freedom, love of mankind, and a search for truth.) Like most revolutions though, people got carried away. The sexual revolution overswung. One consequence was a trivialisation of sex, so that it became like an ice-cream, or a day trip — just another pleasure to sample.

C'MON - JUST A **LITTLE** BIT OF ABSTRACT PHILOSOPHISING

I'M SORRY - I HAPPEN TO BE AN OLD-FASHIONED GIRL WHO DOESN'T BELIEVE IN CONCEPTUALISING BEFORE MARRIAGE

J. WRIGHT

The people who embraced this new freedom told themselves that they could have pleasurable casual sex with anyone who appealed to them at the time, and 'as long as you're honest' everything would be fine (or to use the strikingly accurate jargon of the times, 'cool').

Perhaps the love generation was to some extent a media creation. Were most people a little more careful? Whatever people's actual behaviour, the credo was 'if it feels good do it'. Bodies were to be enjoyed! Before long though, the fallout started. The ideal never matched the experience. Like using heroin, what feels good right now feels very bad later on. Many people found that they were 'getting hurt' almost every time they formed a relationship. Courtship became a competition in *not* feeling or showing sentiment, and the person best at *not* feeling was the winner. Since behind the casualness was a deep yearning for real intimacy (which by the new rules you could never admit), it was a contest in which everyone lost. One of the players would feel they were the loser, and come away reinforcing broken-heartedness as a life position. The other player superficially had won, but was alone again all the same.

Often women found themselves caught in a new double standard — it was 'hip' to be free loving, but the need to be loved at a deeper level still meant a painful sense of loss when a partner moved on. Men who still carried the 'conquest' mentality (of the old ethos) found rich harvests, but a growing sense of jadedness and emotional shutting off. Other men who were more open to their need for intimacy, and more able to be tender and invested with their emotions, found the same pain that women experienced, in the shifting and unsafe seas of free love. There was both great freedom and not a little distress for those of us growing through those times!

Today, as the 1980s move into the 1990s, many people are still grappling with this issue. But people see more clearly now. Disillusionment isn't a bad thing, it's just a step towards being more honest, more free of illusion. Our colleagues in the field of couple counselling around the world have found some guidelines that can be simply stated. Firstly, *we cannot compartmentalise our relationships without a cost*. It is not possible to make love to someone you don't like, or don't understand, without making enormous internal divisions — shutting down natural energies and emotions. The pain this leads to is present in many of the people we have talked to as counsellors, and is made worse because the 'cool' ethos still pervades. As you'll have guessed we're not fond of 'cool', it is dangerously close to 'cold'.

Junk sex

Junk food — like pizza, chocolate, potato chips and so on — is usually strong tasting, convenient and quick to obtain, but it is also fatty and non-nutritious. Just as you can live (for a while) on junk food, some people live on *junk sex*. Junk sex has most of the same qualities — it gives instant gratification and leaves a bad taste in your mouth. It's quick and easy, and that's about all. Junk sex is not limited to singles or kids either. Many long-standing couples have given up on a roast and just settle for a pizza!

The phrase *making love* has come to endure in our language because it describes so poetically an ideal we all seek. When you get sexuality right, making love is exactly what you are doing. Your heart opens (softens), your genitals open (enliven), your mind opens (sharpens and sparkles), to let the other person in. Achieving this is rarely rapid, and can hardly be temporary. *If you have once made LOVE, then just 'making sex' will never do.*

Love is not an affliction or a hole one 'falls' into, it is a flame which a skilful human being learns to kindle. Love may strike us fortuitously like lightning, so that the flame comes as a gift, but it is then up to us to cultivate this gift. We can never guarantee this flame or take it for granted. We do, however, learn to fuel and intensify its glow. In a day-to-day relationship the flame flickers, dies down, flares up, and sways in the wind, as we learn to manage it well. Our efforts are rewarded. Love starts as a blessing, even a fluke, but it continues as an accomplishment.

Couples aren't everything

Sometimes in the excitement of becoming a couple, people make a serious mistake — they forget about their friends. The role of friends in making life happier and easier has been grossly devalued in our culture, resulting in much loneliness and pain. Friendships for a time came to be seen as almost a casual thing — people to fill in time with until one found one's 'true love'. The family was all-encompassing, met all needs. Friends were just people to chat to at barbecues, and have over to dinner. For a woman, perhaps one single good friendship was acceptable; for men there were often only the most superficial peer relationships. At the height of this phase, vividly described in Philip Slater's book *The Pursuit of Loneliness*, we simply discovered the dramatic fact that the couple or the family in isolation does not work. A family without friends is about as stable as a tent without guy ropes.

Fortunately we learn quickly. The steep rise in both marriage break-ups and single parenthood soon led people to re-examine the lonely way in which we had closeted our lives. The lack of friends placed too much strain on couples and left too few support networks in the event of a return to singleness. Recently the tide has turned. Close friendships, across age, sex and other boundaries, are being resurrected as a central part of social life.

For a couple starting out in shared life, the lesson is simple. Don't abandon your friends in the rush of couplehood. And don't marry someone who expects that in exchange for love, you should drop all your friends. One way or another, you're going to need them.

We have covered the nature and variety of attraction, but one question remains: why do we choose a particular person to be our partner? What draws us to one person and not another? And why is it worth persisting when things become difficult?

You Marry Your Twin

You marry your what?

This surprising and illuminating idea is gaining much favour among couple therapists around the world. The theory states that attraction is largely unconscious — we are drawn to hidden traits, as much as obvious ones. So people who differ on the surface but are very similar deep down, will be inexorably drawn into couple relationships. Think about your own partner now. You will be aware of your differences but your similarities will, for the most part, be unconscious. You may be actively denying having the traits which your partner has — both virtues, and vices. The possibility is strong that these aspects are equally in your make-up too. This has a neat circular logic to it. The theory actually predicts that you will disagree with it vehemently in your own case, though you may see it operating in other couples! Let's examine this 'twinness' more closely.

As couples, we have a strong investment in seeing our partner as totally different to us. Couples will joke about how different they are: 'I leave the money to her'; 'He's the one with the brains'; 'She's so emotional'; 'He's irresponsible, impulsive — I can't let him out of my sight'. Also, when things are going badly, these differences are given even more airplay. The truth is, nonetheless, that *likes* attract.

As we grow from childhood, much of our so-called character development is regrettably not positive, but rather the shutting down of certain faculties. For instance our clear brains, intuition, patience, spontaneity, or emotionality, may have proved to be too risky and at odds with what the adults around us could handle. The reproductive process of learning to fit in leads to our eventual self-image as dumb, confused, unimaginative, bad tempered, cautious, or moody, and so on. We emerge as adults who in distinctive ways, have shut down aspects of our capacity to think, feel and act. (It's interesting that someone who is less 'shut down' than is the norm, and who is expressive and flowing in thought, feeling, action, we refer to quite accurately as having 'lots of personality'. We all have lots of personality [on the inside] but may be afraid to let it show.)

We begin searching for a partner at an age when we are just beginning to take shape as an adult. As we seek out the right partner for us, we are seeking, largely unconsciously, to balance ourselves, by locating someone *who is still activated in the areas we have shut down*. Think of what qualities attract you most in a partner. Outgoingness, humour, gentleness, commitment to strong values, emotional honesty, physical health and energy, creativity, sexuality, and so on. Which are the ones that most appeal to you? After all, there is no universal scale for attractiveness. The recent fad for rating people on a scale of ten is debasing and silly. Attraction is a combination of the needs and potentials of both people involved.

This is the secret behind all kinds of interpersonal attraction, including heroes we admire, as well as just friends. *We are attracted to people largely because they have something that we unconsciously know that we have too.* If you hold someone in great admiration, this is because you have the capacity to be like that person too, and this creates the yearning which we call admiration. If this potential wasn't also dormant in you, you would not even notice the qualities of the other person, they simply would not register. (An old Sufi joke says that when a pickpocket meets a saint, all he notices are his pockets. We would want to add, when a half-saint meets a saint, they see what they might one day be.)

> Stan and Eileen are as different as you could imagine. He is a truck driver and union organiser. Eileen is a nurse specialising in infant health. He appears brusque and tough, and he is. She is small and pretty and moves and speaks with incredible gentleness. One can picture how they would have looked in their wedding photos. But that was twenty-five years ago now, and they have developed as people. In raising children and exploring their relationship together, each has activated the qualities of the other. Stan is also, when the need arises, soft and gentle. His handling of industrial disputes has become balanced and effective. Problems get solved, people find themselves co-operating. In addition, if his wife is away interstate, he can take a phone call from a distressed parent in the early hours and people assume the nurse's husband must be a doctor! Eileen has also 'rounded out', and is tough and piercing when meeting with a child-abusing father or a doctor not doing his job.

We are drawn, then, to a partner who, at depth, is very like us, but who, on the surface, shows parts that we do not yet own up to in ourselves. These facets can be qualities which are a plus, such as being loving, emotionally warm, powerful, confident and so on, or a minus, like being dependent, domineering, unreliable and so on. Psychoanalysts and others who like big words call this 'projective identification'. The key is, that *whatever we see in them, we have too* (at least potentially). Whether what we are aware of in our partner is a quality we admire, or a fault we dislike, the first step is to own up to it in ourself. This is the true meaning of *tolerance*. It is not just 'putting up' with other people's natures, but realising that we and they are the same. Acknowledging even the possibility of unowned and as yet unintegrated parts of our nature is what human growth is all about.

This is also the reason why we are so intolerant of certain faults in others — not just the normal dislike of sloppiness, or singing in the shower, or the way they keep tidying up, but the intense irritations that we sometimes feel about certain behaviour. The more we repress in ourself, the more intolerant we are of others. Some of this originates in the vigorous criticism of our parents which we develop in the teenage years. It is as if we have to rebel against them, but in doing so deny that we could ever 'be like that'.

One patient of ours reacted with enormous hurt and anger when his wife mentioned one day that his breath smelled. It seemed that he had spent his adolescence in a crowded apartment, in almost constant conflict with his father. His father was by all accounts a very smelly individual, and this trait became the focus of all the son's dislike and rejection. His psychic survival as a teenager meant rejecting any similarity to his (odorous) old man! The passage from teenager to adult requires a softening of such black and white divisions. We are all human, and we all smell funny if allowed to deteriorate! Our patient needed to know that he would not turn into his father just because he ate blue vein cheese, or forgot to clean his teeth occasionally. Also to forgive his father for not being everything he could hope for. There comes a time to stop sulking.

How couple relationships show us ourselves

When we are drawn to a quality in our loved one, we need also to realise that we can eventually activate that potential in ourselves. When we balk at a fault in our partner, we need to look at how we too have exactly the same fault, though perhaps expressed in other ways. As the relationship unfolds, we are soon brought into contact with parts of ourselves that we may have trouble 'owning'. Worse still, the very things which attracted us to our partner in the first place will often prove to be a stumbling block at a later stage. A client of ours, Ian, writes:

> I liked Kristina's extroversion, and her easy-going nature right from the start. Unlike me, she never worried about tomorrow, and was generous and open hearted with money and time. But after our marriage, this became more and more a source of tension. I would worry about our financial security — she could waste a week's income on a gift for a sick friend. It reached a point where I thought our

relationship would come to a painful end. All my happiness was at stake, because I could not shake off my uptightness about money and security. I resolved to give it one more try, and to actually change my own habitual reactions. Against my better judgement, I went along with her impulses, enjoyed and encouraged her projects. We took a holiday together which I had protested we couldn't afford. At the same time, I made sure that she had information on our bank and credit card balances (which I had previously taken care of without wanting to worry her). I even had a few impulsive but enjoyable outbursts myself. I found that I was becoming more relaxed, and that paradoxically, Kristina started telling me how much she had saved that week, and that she thought we should keep some money back for the future, to which I naturally agreed.

Ian was a brave man, and we were relieved for him that he had found a new balance. He had generosity hidden in *his* nature, and his wife had responsibility just waiting to emerge in *hers*.

Marrying one's 'twin' means that working through couple problems and challenges is enormously self-liberating, if you persist. It's also the reason why many people leave their partner — when they come up against something they cannot handle in themselves. Then they find another 'twin' and repeat the cycle again. By cutting out of a relationship whenever the same issue resurfaces, one can spend a lifetime without ever facing up to oneself. This is not a weakness, but just indicates a lack of support and insight needed for more rapid progress.

Steven and Ondrea Levine, American teachers of Buddhism, spoke at a recent conference about how the object of marriage is *not* to centre one's life around the other person. According to the Levines, the object of all life's activities is to find the truth. However, two people seeking their own true selves, while in a committed relationship, find a companionship on the path, which immeasurably speeds and enriches their journey. Your partner is a mirror in which to get to know yourself! Coupling is powerful magic. Meditate in a cave for twenty years, or plan your summer vacation, the result is the same — you'll either get enlightenment or go crazy!

How to find the partner for you?

A brief word on finding your partner, if you are currently alone. We believe there is a right partner for everyone who wants one. If you are anguished by the search for a good life companion, we suggest you first take a long look at whether you really want someone now, and are available to love — in a practical, committed, step by step sense. Being fully available yourself produces not only openness and beauty, but an irresistible energetic attraction. The flower attracts the bee by flowering, while the bee finds the flower by beeing!

Time and again we've found that when men or women finally decide that they want a partner, they very quickly find one. Sometimes the hold-up is caused by not letting go of an old relationship. A person, 'hanging on' to an old relationship (even holding on to hurts is, after all, still holding on), who finally says goodbye fully to the past is invariably surprised to find someone new literally knocking on his or her door.

A lovely and capable forty-year-old woman friend of ours recently came to a sudden realisation that she has been 'beating around the bush' for years, never allowing herself to 'want what she wanted'. She had spent years in heart-rending pursuit of dreams and fantasies, a guaranteed way to disappointment. Finally realising how alone she was, and how lonely her future looked, she decided in the shower one day 'Damn it! I want a man, and I want a job!'. Within weeks she had found both a job, and a wonderful life companion. Love is not in short supply on this planet. Be yourself, like yourself, and your twin will be there.

There is a key attitude to take with you in the search for a partner. It is written into your face, your words, your stance, and your walk. It may as well be written like a T-shirt slogan across your chest. It is a statement of belief in your loveability.

Some people wear an invisible T-shirt which gives out a message almost like a puppy, or a small child. It says 'Please love me'. This T-shirt may get you a mama or a daddy, but not a mature, equal-sharing lover. Some people go the other way. Their T-shirt reads 'I don't need your love!'. This is, of course, true, but why say so? A fiercely guarded palace indicates a scared king or queen inside!

So what is the winning T-shirt message? It has small, but clear writing, on a strong background. It says 'I *am worth loving*'. Those who read your T-shirt message may or may not choose to take it up. You may choose whether or not they qualify!

Contracts: The Freedom You Can Count On

People today can choose to live in many different kinds of couple-relationships. You may be married, or be live-in lovers, or committed but unmarried life-partners, or occasional lovers, or just good friends. In any of these combinations you can be just starting out together, or evolving from one form to another, or be in a process of separation.

So there is great freedom, and great potential for confusion. The problem isn't in how it's described to others, but in the two people themselves understanding what they are doing together. It's essential to know what the relationship means to the other party, and if it has the same meaning for you. This shared understanding is what we call 'the contract' — what we expect of the other, and what they expect of us.

In all our relationships in life, there are agreements (usually unspoken) as to how people will behave. If you wave to a friend you see in the street, you expect that he or she will wave back. That is what a relationship means — a sense of continuity in expected behaviour. We need to know that, in certain key ways, we can count on each other. A deep contract such as that between partners requires time to evolve. The paradox of contracts is that they actually make us freer, since we know exactly where we stand. A contract in a couple relationship doesn't need to restrict freedom, it just means that freedoms have to be agreed on.

Contracts exist between every couple, and most misunderstandings that couples have are basically contractual in origin. Whether or not the 'terms' are actually discussed, (or even thought about), is immaterial. Developing a contract that is right for you is therefore a big step towards happiness in life.

How contracts are made

Contracts start being established and tested out very soon in a relationship: we find out about our partner's reliability in keeping dates, we resolve issues about spending money, we decide how much time to spend together. These things may be discussed or simply happen, but they are very much on our minds. We soon move on to solving questions about going out with other people, and expected sexual behaviour. They eventually may cover important areas such as sexual faithfulness, affection, financial support, responsibilities for children, time-allocation, and so on.

Couples in the past often found out what their contract was only after it had been broken, after someone had stepped across the invisible line in the expectations of the other person! In the old days there was a well-defined pattern of courtship, betrothal and wedding banns. People knew how to behave. These days we often lack even the words to express what we are about.

'Well, if you really cared about me you wouldn't . . .'
'Wouldn't what?'
'Well, you know . . . I thought we were, you know, together.'
'You mean going steady?'
'Don't laugh!'

Evolving a contract that's right for you

It is important to realise that *there is nothing wrong with having rules and expectations of each other.* (In fact it is impossible not to have them.) The only wrong we can do is in not making these wishes explicit.

Our primary responsibility to each other is two sided:
– to be honest about our needs and expectations, and
– to only make commitments we intend to keep.

Couples whom we've talked to find it enormously useful and reassuring to discuss firstly what their contract actually is, and secondly whether it is in fact what each wants. A contract is an individual and changing thing, fitting to a couple's unique needs, personalities, ages, and changing circumstance. (In *The Secret of Happy Children* we mentioned the couple in their nineties, who couldn't stand the sight of each other, but had waited to get divorced 'until their children had died!')

If you are wary of contracts, then make them short term. For instance a couple having trouble resolving conflicts (for fear of breaking up) may contract to stay together for six months, whatever happens. Couples who make the 'modern' choice of living together for a time often benefit greatly from discussion of contracts, since they can then form a unique contract that suits them, instead of slipping into a vague or unsatisfying arrangement which may delay their fulfilment (if it later emerges that they actually had quite different needs).

Many people we talk to are afraid of making a commitment. At the heart of it, they fear being caught in conflict and distress which cannot be resolved. So people elect to be uncommitted and lonely, rather than risk being emotionally or financially trapped. There is a wide range of options in between though!

Contracting starts simply with communication about what we like and want in life. It seems extraordinarily good sense to start early and head off misunderstandings, and to form shared beliefs. Major issues can be dealt with later as the relationship grows: sexual ethics, roles in the family, time allocation, and so on. Minor aspects of our contracts will be changed and constantly renegotiated through the life cycle.

Expressions like 'devotion', 'commitment', or promises of 'in sickness and in health, for richer for poorer', although old-fashioned, are often what people crave deep down. When our generation rejected traditional ideas of marriage, it sought to replace a social form with a genuine experience. This is a revolutionary thing to do, and requires some effort. It means taking gradual steps. We begin with the intentional choice of commitment, of deciding to 'have a go'. If this commitment is time-limited to begin with, that's okay, for you have to start somewhere. Next comes the experience of pushing on through difficult times, when without commitment it seems easier to simply give up. We discover that storms can be weathered, that conflicts can be solved, that we can trust our partner, and trust ourself! Eventually, our commitment develops from being a wish and an intention, into a bond which is heartfelt and vigorous. This shift is often unnoticed. We have been watching the waves, while gradually in came the tide.

To have security, with freedom to be oneself, is a universal wish. Fulfilment of this wish is available to anyone who seeks it, and is willing to do the work.

Beyond the couple

As we will explore in the following chapters, the effects of loving don't stop within the couple, but flow on naturally into the world around. Loving a partner is far from an insular journey. Although at first the bond deepens upon itself, it soon blossoms out into family and community. Couple energy may produce children, it also sustains them and wraps them in a wordless security. Rather than becoming inward and narcissistic, mature couples find they have energy to spare (especially at the 'heart' level, the sense of liking and generosity). As your life together deepens, the greatest pleasure lies in caring for the family your love generates, and the human race that you now feel so much more a part of.

CHAPTER 3

Deepening Contact

He: *I get so angry when she goes her own way in things.*

We: *You get what?*

He: *I get really furious.*

We: *Is that what's happening right now as you talk about it? Notice what you're feeling . . .*

He: *My chest is tight, my heart's beating fast. Isn't that anger?*

We: *No.*

He: *Well, . . . yeah . . . scared I suppose.*

We: *Ahh . . . tell that to her now . . .*

Keep on Talking

We talk for two reasons only: to solve problems and to organise fulfilment. All human language has evolved to this end. The famous psychiatrist and writer Eric Berne claimed that we only need three words to carry out our relationships: Yes, No, and Wow! For most of us, however, communication requires a little more detail.

Couples can have two basic kinds of communication problems. They may either talk too much and not get anywhere, which means that they aren't saying what they really need to, or they may hardly

talk at all, perhaps having tried and then given up through lack of a good outcome. To have a 'living' relationship, and create happiness from day to day, you will need to know how to talk straight, how to fight clean, and when to stop talking and do something. (Run, tickle, throw things, dig the garden, make love and so on).

Talking itself isn't what helps, it's how you talk, or as they say 'where you come from'. Let's explore this aspect first. There is a simple system called transactional analysis which is helpful in simplifying confused communication. In this system, you can divide your personality into three parts as follows:

Your many parts

The Child

This part you were born with. It's the part of your personality that has all of the wants and feelings, the impulses and the self-interest, the fun and the energy. Your Child department can be beautiful and child*like*, or sometimes (through being mishandled), exasperating and child*ish*.

The Parent

The second part of your personality was acquired while you were growing up, by your brain's memory cells literally recording the big people around you: 'Gee you're stupid'; 'Big boys don't cry'; 'You are so beautiful'; 'Eat your vegetables' and so on. These deep unexamined messages become a lasting influence, although they are not even historically accurate (since little children often misunderstand).

This collection of tape recordings (Mum and Dads' Greatest Hits) which form your internal Parent can be kind, gentle and non-possessive, or harsh, blaming and intrusive, depending on your upbringing. Usually you come out with a mixture. Some irrational hangups and some saving graces!

Even as early as age two, the growing human being will have an active Parent department up and running in their mind. It'll be added to, but the foundations have taken shape. Obviously having a mind with both Child feelings and wants on one side and Parent shoulds, ought tos and don't-you-dares on the other, makes for much internal conflict. You can have most of your arguments inside your own head.

The Adult

To save your mind from being in constant civil war you also develop (if you're lucky), a third part called the Adult — the ability to think and reason. The hassles which normal two-year-olds have are not just purposeless conflict. This is the time when the child starts developing this Adult capacity to figure things out. That's why some frustration of wants is essential at this age so the capacity to reason, compromise and delay can begin to be internalised.

Once the growing child is equipped with all three 'voices', they can begin to function in an increasingly mature way. What they want, what they should do and what's reasonable and going to succeed, can all be weighed up. A child slowly becomes self-asserting, and yet moral, and skilful. At least that's the theory! In practice it takes a while to get all three sorted out. By the time you are grown up and ready to relate to other adults, you are in the midst of a continual, wonderfully complex internal dialogue with yourself.

The Adult does not rule the roost, but it often steps in to save the day. The Adult part of your mind reasons its way between Child impulses and Parent restrictions, and enables you to get on with life.

Child:	I'd love that cheesecake-
Parent:	You'll get fat.
Adult:	It has 200 calories. If I walk the dog tonight and brush my teeth I should be okay.

When your parts meet theirs!

Now, we are ready to look at couple communication. The combination of two people, each with a choice of three 'departments' from which to respond, gives a lot of flexibility. If 'coming from' one part of your makeup gets you an unsatisfactory response, you can try another until it works out.

Most couples find that certain areas of discussion or topics of conversation always seem to bog down — that the problem refuses to go away, that every time it is discussed they get nowhere. Worse still, after a while they can almost predict to a word what the other person is going to say, making it both exasperating and boring!

This is where some quick transactional analysis can be of great help in getting unstuck. If you can determine which part you habitually 'come from' in these discussions, and change this to one of the other two, then new possibilities can occur.

Being who you want to be

Unless your childhood was extremely disturbed, you will have all three aspects — Parent, Adult and Child — available to you. The proportions though, will vary greatly from person to person. Some people habitually stay in their Parent, and as a result live a life full of rules and restrictions, shoulds and ought tos. Another kind of 'over-parental' person is continually very giving and caring to others, but not to him or herself. Others are Adult to the point of boringness, though certainly well organised and competent. Others are delightfully, (or exasperatingly) full of Child energy. The problem comes when people restrict themselves, as if they have a big house but always stay in the basement, or the attic, or the living room.

Few people realise that this is going on, since they are unaware of, or discount the importance of, their other parts. This imbalance affects all our relationships, but none more critically than our choice of a life partner. In fact our balance of parts influences (a) *whom we choose* as a partner, and (b) *how you both get along* once the choice is made.

For example, you may have been attracted to your current spouse because he or she had a lovely free Child (pity about the drinking) or a reassuringly nurturing Parent (but a bit boring in bed!), and so on. Fortunately most of the reasons why we are attracted to a certain person are the positive ones, for we tend to choose a partner who complements and promotes the very best parts of us.

The important point in all this is that, since everyone has all three parts, we can each choose from moment to moment how we wish to interact. What determines your fulfilment or frustration is where you both choose to 'come from', and how these fit together. When people are being free there is great choice and flexibility, and it is possible to slip from clear Adult to playful Child to caring strong Parent as you wish and as the need arises.

The key is to mix 'your three' and theirs in ways which complement and satisfy. There are four distinct ways to 'get along well', all of which you'll likely recognise and appreciate.

The Four Cs of Couple Communication

'Caring': Parent → Child

Everyone needs to depend, and be cared for, and receive nurturance, from time to time. There is nothing quite like knowing that another person wants your happiness. Couples often begin like this: kindness of word, and touch, and thoughtfulness, are very much a part of courtship behaviour. When we fall in love, such actions are easy to offer and received appreciatively. Later many couples may become less giving, and worse still, devalue what is routinely given, as if it is simply to be expected, or part of some unspoken contract. There is an enduring phrase for this — 'being taken for granted'.

Ask for nurturance in straight ways, by negotiation. For instance consider spending time receiving non-sexual massage, preparing a meal for the other person, listening to your partner talk things out, which do not directly concern you, but they have a need to air. There is such a thing as overweaning, even intrusive fussing over one's partner, but this is usually a one-way process, and does not endure for long. Some couples unwittingly follow an old stereotype by which all the nurturing is done by the woman for the man, (who has 'brought home the bacon', and so need do nothing else!). Okay, if that's the contract, but it is not a way to foster closeness. Be sure to care for one another interchangeably, not always one way.

Also (in our society) caring is often only given (or received) in connection with ill health and injury. As a result people in need of care often hurt or neglect themselves and so earn caring by acquiring real ill health. A vast health 'care' industry has grown up to meet often basically psychological needs for nurturance.

Giving and receiving, one being the Parent, another the Child, even if only for fleeting moments, is the currency of closeness and allows a naturalness and comfort to permeate one's day-to-day life.

Compatibility: Parent → Parent

Talk over values, beliefs, aspirations, childraising issues, and so on, in an exploratory way, not waiting until something is a practical issue. By talking and thinking out aloud, we develop a common ground about where our lives are going, and what we see as being of value. There is no need to struggle for agreement — simply airing and exploring ideas will lead to a meshing of paths. Think of trees in a rainforest. Slowly over decades their roots and branches mesh, yet they always remain distinct and different. Thus individual goals can be known and reached in more or less complete harmony with the other person. There is enhancement of each other's goals for a life fully lived.

Couples may go for a long time without ever talking about the really big questions (such as 'what are we doing with our lives!'). Some people find that they make use of long car trips together in this way, talking about long-range ideas and thoughts that there is seldom a chance to discuss amidst the day-to-day demands of home life. Certain events or experiences can trigger a re-examination: when we first saw the film *The Big Chill* we sat up almost until dawn talking about where we had been and where we were going.

Compatibility isn't a perfect 'fit' like pieces of a jigsaw puzzle — it's an ongoing style of communicating, a way of processing differences and changes constantly so that our lives support each other's goals, gaining strength without compromise or loss of scope for either.

Contracting: Adult → Adult

Much of day-to-day life is simply a matter of practicalities. Why not make the business of making transport arrangements, allocating money, shopping, schooling, childcare, chores and who will do what and when an easy process, by doing it with skill.

Keep this kind of thing unemotional and objective. Pay attention to detail, so that things are smoother and easier in the long run. Be trustworthy. Make lists, detail needs, explore options, strike bargains, negotiate compromises, and so on. You can be friendly, and kind, while dealing from your Adult, but keep the focus always on the facts.

Have you noticed how some people carry out their day-to-day lives with a certain unpleasant flavour always coming through? By flavour, we mean a quality that they add to complicate what would otherwise be simple. For instance, some people flavour their housework with an additive called 'harassed', or 'guilty', or 'resentful'. If you enjoy 'getting even' with the dishes, or 'taking it out' on the carpet, or 'fighting' the traffic to get the kids to school, don't let us stop you! But in negotiating these things with each other, remember that they are simply arrangements. How you choose to feel doesn't change the task. Learn to make agreements, and do what you've promised. Be prepared to keep altering the contract until it suits.

Contracts also include larger issues, like monogamy, honesty about money, being reliable about contraception and life-affecting behaviour like drinking, drugs and vehicle safety. Trust has to be proven, and broken trust has to be re-earned twice over. People who don't know how to keep their word are not ready for adult relationships.

Closeness: Child → Child

By this we mean simply playing together. Closeness includes. all fun and recreation together, all exchanges of affection, and of course sex. Many couples enjoy just being companionably around each other in the garden or house at weekends. Some parts of this will include play with the kids, but it's important to always have closeness that is just as a couple too. Closeness and fun are the ways in which your energy is regenerated.

Many people who grew up in tough times did not learn to play easily — there was neither the time, the opportunity, or the example. Playfullness is a skill and requires some risk taking. You may find that you and your partner are a great work-team — renovating half-a-dozen houses, raising half-a-dozen kids, making a million dollars, but never stopping to just 'be'. Well done, but consider the other side of life while there is time, and the pleasure that comes just from walking in the sunshine.

Touch is of special importance. Personally we are often astounded at how easily and quickly a gentle, stroking touch can change one's whole state of mind for the better. The need for touch is as real as hunger or thirst, and as perennial.

For closeness to succeed, couples need to distinguish, too, between the need for affectionate touch, and the distinctly different energy of sexual touching. One kind may flow into the other, but they meet a different appetite, and it is important to be clear about what you need.

So, in this way of describing things, we have four clear and distinct ways of being together. A fulfilling partnership involves moving easily from one mode to another as the need arises.

> Ed and Edna wake up in the morning and snuggle together for a while. They watch carefully as a moth flies across the ceiling.
>
> 'You'd better get it' says Ed, 'it's on your side of the bed'.
>
> 'No', says Edna, 'that's your job. I'm in charge of primary industry, you're in charge of defence!' Ed jumps up after the moth, but bangs himself on a heater beside the bed. The moth has disappeared. He comes back to bed, crestfallen, and Edna comforts him. Soon the sound of youngsters stirring in the next room reaches their ears.
>
> 'Well, another day!' says Ed. Edna is already getting out of bed, stretching. The four Cs have already taken place and it's only 7 a.m. And Ed and Edna are only cats! Humans are even better!

Here is a checklist which will help you to use the four Cs of couple communication. You can use a fingernail if you don't have a pen handy.

Four Cs Questionnaire

Consider the following, and indicate to what degree you think you are connecting with your partner through:

Caring (giving to, and nurturing of, each in turn)

(you giving)	very little ☐	some ☐	plenty ☐
(you receiving)	very little ☐	some ☐	plenty ☐

Compatibility (of values, beliefs, aspirations)

very little ☐	some ☐	plenty ☐

Contracting (logical making of arrangements)

very little ☐	some ☐	plenty ☐

Closeness (playful or emotionally expressive contact)

very little ☐   some ☐   plenty ☐

The other need of a person in a couple is to not always be part of a couple, to have a sense of breathing space, as a separate and complete growing self. Could you add this last self assessment to those above?

Self-reliance (to what degree you can enjoy your own separateness)

very little ☐   some ☐   plenty ☐

      (to what degree you can accept your partner's separateness)

very little ☐   some ☐   plenty ☐

From completing the above, it will be very clear to you what's there for you, and what's not there, in your relationship at the moment. Having this 'map' will make it much easier to find your way. You may want to talk about this with your partner and find out how it is for him or her. If there are changes you want, be sure to emphasise the positive, and stay in your own Adult as you talk about how it can benefit you both.

Letting Go of Patterns You No Longer Need

Compatibility, caring, contracting and closeness are all needed for a flowing, sustaining relationship. Too much of any one can become a problem. Sometimes people get stuck in one mode of being, and don't move beyond it. Let's expand on how this happens.

The rescuing trap: where would you be without me?

The Parent → Child nurturing dimension in a couple's lives should usually be a reversible arrangement, so there is a balanced amount of give and take when averaged out over time. If it becomes too one-way, then this is called a rescuing relationship. Here's an example. These are real people, using real names, and every detail is absolutely true.

Eric was a bank clerk. He lived alone in an immaculate but rather bare flat, drove a second-hand Saab, and stayed at home at nights programming his computer. He always had his income tax done on time. His friends worried about him (he was twenty-six and nearly over the hill) and they invited him out to parties when they remembered. Eric went along as it seemed the right thing to do.

At one such party, Eric couldn't help noticing Darlene. In fact no-one could help noticing Darlene. She laughed a lot, touched people when she spoke to them, and wore not quite enough clothes! Somehow Darlene and Eric were introduced, and talked a little, and when Eric went home that night, she stayed foremost in his thoughts. Darlene too found herself thinking about the quiet, tidy, shy young man, and since she did not suffer inhibitions in such matters, soon got his phone number from some mutual friends.

What happened next was one of those things that happen once or twice in a lifetime and make you wonder about the universe. Darlene decided to take steps. She dialled Eric's number, and at that very second, some distance away across the moonlit night, Eric decided to call her. He lifted the phone, and before he could punch a number, there she was. Within weeks they were engaged, within months married, and nobody could have been happier. At least to begin with.

If we stop to analyse the combination here, you can see that the couple certainly complement each other — in fact too well. Eric provides the Adult sense and Parent responsibility. Darlene provides the Child vitality. Between the two of them, Darlene and Eric make up *one whole person*! This is dependency all right, but who is depending on whom? And, will it last?

Eric has very little fun unless Darlene is around. Darlene is very insecure unless Eric organises her life. So in a sense they *rescue* each other. You'll probably know old couples where one really appears to be like a Child and the other more like a Parent. (Though again don't be fooled, the dependency is mutual.) If one partner dies then often the other just fades away too. We wouldn't criticise this arrangement for one minute, for it can work very well. In the old days this kind of arrangement worked better, however, for while people still matured, they did so like a cheese, slowly and evenly, and rarely underwent the kinds of dramatic changes that are now commonplace.

Today there is a great deal of self-exploration, and there are opportunities for people to change direction and unfold their personalities. As a result individuals often change greatly in the course of a lifetime. So what will happen to Eric and Darlene if one starts to grow? What will happen if Eric learns to have fun, and spends their holiday money on skis, or Darlene goes to college and starts to develop her serious side, and invents a better computer program than Eric? Either way, someone is going to be put out.

In the example of Eric and Darlene, the woman took the Child role. Another rescuing variation could have the man with a large Child component, for example, an alcoholic, with a wife who forgives and covers up for him, but nags and criticises too, and generally runs things from her Parent. A workaholic follows the same pattern, although of course work is more respectable!

The trouble with these co-rescuing arrangements is that developments like strength, growth, and self-reliance are often perceived as an attack on the relationship. We know of a number of alcoholics, as well as war veterans, depressed people, agoraphobics, and so on, whose partners have had serious initial problems caused by them getting well!

Competing— the contest where everyone loses

The second trap to avoid is competing. This is where neither partner will nurture because '*I need it more than you do*'. Whatever role one partner takes, (usually Parent or Child), the other goes to the same position and tries to outdo the other in intensity.

'I've had a dreadful day' . . .	'You've had a bad day You ought to try being home with three screaming kids.'
'Your friends are so boring' . . .	'Well at least they don't drop in uninvited like yours do.'
'I've got a headache' . . .	'Me too. And I can feel my flu coming back as well.'

Competing couples come for counselling a lot, and they usually come together. They want to be sure the other partner doesn't put anything over them and they want the counsellor to keep score!

A little competing can be fun, but a lot is often very sad. No-one gets anything much. Children suffer. Competition between adult partners is like two kids fighting over a fragile toy: the toy breaks and everyone loses. Competing is based on the idea that love is in short supply, that there's not enough to go around. Perhaps this was true back in each partner's childhood experience. But as adults there is plenty of love once we learn how to generate it. And unlike cake or candy, the more love you give away, the more you get back. Later in this chapter we'll teach you how to get all that you need in a relationship, while giving all that your partner needs.

The disengaged couple

The third and final couple type in our range don't come for counselling very often on their own account. Usually it's the children's problems that bring them along. Disengaged couples are people who have given up on closeness (and sometimes even on talking at all).

'My husband? Oh, I think he's home somewhere. Just a second and I'll ask one of the kids.'

'My wife? Yes, I wrote her a cheque the other day. I've got the receipt here.'

A disengaged relationship can be amicable and very productive, and yet somehow there is a missing 'heart' to things.

Jonathon and Fran spoke openly in a workshop of ours about how they lived 'separate lives' for over thirty years, and while never being truly content, they raised happy children, and were productive and secure. The death of their daughter in a light plane crash broke through the barrier of separation. Each parent's grief switched into anger at the other, over missed opportunities and long stored misunderstandings. Communication that was previously cool but courteous now disappeared entirely. Jonathon sought out other relationships, something he had never done before. Fran prepared to leave and live alone. Somehow in the midst of all this, and they were never quite sure how, the two began to experience the depth of feeling that existed between them, and simply grew close. Their discovery of a long denied intimacy worked wonders for both. Now in their sixties their glowing faces and their healthy, mobile bodies would be the envy of many couples of lesser years.

In a disengaged state, a pair may continue to live together, but do not 'connect'. Perhaps this is just forgetfulness. There are stages when, for many couples, the demands of living, and especially of parenting, become so much the focus that they simply forget to be partners. Sometimes people can be good parents even though they are non-partners. Earlier generations accepted this as the norm — that one lived in a marriage arrangement and did not expect much real closeness or communication. (But males and females are like opposing magnets, and they will not drift around loose for long. The mistress, or recurrent affairs, were common in the days of the loveless marriage.) And sexual needs aside, it is hard to be a parent, trying to be a source of love, when there is none flowing in.

Couples don't start out disengaged. 'Wanna come and live with me and we won't talk to each other?' is hardly a winning proposal! Disengaged couples have usually fled from either rescuing or competing, and not found another way to closeness. When they try to engage, each connection turns quickly into bitterness (competitive), or overweaning (rescuing), so that they pull back in uncertainty as to how to proceed.

Disengagement sometimes sets in for a time before eventually leading to a separation. Studies have recently indicated that many separating couples, far from the old stereotypes of vindictiveness and bitterness, simply move apart in a sensible, reasonably co-operative way, and remain friendly and even-handed ever after. Or if there is a fighting phase, this is a part of the resolution, and leads to peaceful closure, with beneficial learning for future life.

Free up and flow on

As you've been reading the above, you may have been deciding 'what you are' as a couple: rescuing, competing or disengaged. Whatever you decided, don't! Most couples experience all three at times, in a mixture together with the healthier ways of connecting. But you are not your patterns! We point out these patterns, and exaggerate them with some tongue in cheek, to help you abandon them for the melodramas they in fact are.

Everyone gets stuck from time to time. The key is to notice it sooner and sooner, until it just doesn't happen any more. The advantage of stuckness is, it's beautifully predictable! When people get stuck, it is invariably in one of the three ways we've described. Eventually you recognise it, and get so bored or angry that you break out. All we are doing here is hoping to save you a decade or three.

Why do we get stuck at all? Are human beings stupid or something? Yes and no! When you are in a car that gets bogged, the more you rev, the more bogged you become. When things are not working in a relationship, people who are rescuing will rescue harder, people who compete will compete harder, and disengaged couples will separate further! Family therapist Moshe Lang has a beautiful way of summing up this human tendency to do more of what doesn't work. He quotes the man who said 'I've been boiling this egg for hours and it's *still* hard!'.

A breaking out story

The way out of an old pattern is to change your responses deliberately. Almost anything you do, different from what you usually do, will help get things changing. Go back again and look at the four Cs, and experiment gently with expanding the aspect that you think is missing most. Do this in a generous way. Be prepared to put out some energy to make change possible. Everyone is changing all the time. Each chapter of this book will offer you ways to speed up this process. Sometimes on the great highway of life, a short cut turns out to be a dead-end. You don't grit your teeth and drive in circles! You turn around, come out again, and look for a new way ahead.

This seems a good place to include, as an illustration, a letter from a colleague of ours, a man in his early thirties, who was generous enough to let us share his unique experience with others.

Four or five years ago, my wife became increasingly unwell, with a condition which doctors took very seriously, but could suggest no treatment for. Chronic mononucleosis, myalgic encephelo-myelitis, immune disorders and glandular fever were all suggested and tested for, with the inconclusive results that these disorders apparently attract. There was nothing vague about the effects though, and she experienced fatigue, weight loss, and nausea enough to have to suspend her studies, and eventually spend some months confined to bed. We were about to embark on the 'interstate specialist trail', at the urging of our GP, when we arrived at a decision. We would instead seek some help from a psychotherapist couple in a nearby city whom we knew were powerful and experienced enough to deal with any 'mind' problems that may be contributing to my wife's condition.

I would want your readers to know that I am a logical and careful man, and not given to 'alternative' or 'psychological' remedies. However by this time we were growing desperate, and willing to go perhaps further into new territory. We spent four days living at their centre, and in the course of that time underwent the most pervasive and radical shift in the course of our lifetimes.

We changed from being vegetarian to eating meat again (in my case for the first time in ten years). We learned simple but powerful meditation and yoga exercises. These things, which I tolerated as an experiment to help my wife, actually had more effect on me! Up until now I had felt sensible, aloof and (patronisingly) tolerant of my wife's condition, while she languished in depression. Now it was my turn to become weak and disoriented, while she became happy and energetic! On returning home the changes continued. I decided to stop my overworked and underpaid private practice, where I spent all day amidst other people's distress and loneliness, and to find more fulfilling work. She became more active and industrious, often in 'womanly' pursuits which she as a feminist had previously eschewed. We progressively changed everything in our physical environment: house, suburb, paintings, style of clothes and so on. We bought quality cars, lived in sunnier places, ate better food, and created beauty within and without. We felt a sudden readiness to be parents, a thought that had previously terrified us, and were soon pregnant.

Perhaps these changes were natural. Perhaps any one factor might have made the difference. We were not of a mind to do controlled studies: our life was falling apart, and with help we fixed it! We leave you, the reader, to make up your own mind. We are simply grateful to be moving forwards again.

Understanding Your Wants

The purpose of communication is to let others know your needs and wants. But what if you don't really know what you need? Or worse still, what you think you want doesn't seem to fulfil you once it has come to fruition? Successful dialogue with your partner or children requires a prior step of self-knowledge. Self-knowledge is not a constant, so that your experience will continue to change. You may find that there is a need for regular shuttling between self-awareness, and self-declaration. Then you are on the way to being very happy.

In even the simplest family interaction, you have to go 'inside' to find out your own response. The answers to self-awareness questions are always available inside you, but you need to know where to look. In this section we'll show you some ways this can be done.

The needs collision, and the 'unfulfilment waltz'

Dave is leaving work late on this particular evening. He hasn't finished what he had hoped to, and has a stack of papers to bring home for later attention. At the car park he finds a new scratch on the paintwork of his car. His drive home is slowed by rain and traffic jams. Arriving at his house, he trips on a tricycle in the shadows, drops papers onto the wet grass, swears as he picks them up, and fumbles with one hand for the front door key.

Diane is inside the house, trying to get three vegetables and some not very good quality chops to all be ready at the same time. The kitchen smells of burned custard, and three children under five squabble noisily and tearfully around her feet.

We interrupt this story to let you guess the outcome. What kind of evening will this couple have? What's going on above is called a needs collision. Both parties have considerable built-up needs, almost identical, for peace and quiet, nurturing and appreciation, rest and recreation. Their evening together will most likely be a contest, the name of the contest being 'who had the worst day'!

Instead of the precious gaps in the evening being filled with supportive or even practical gestures, there is likely to be a fight over who most deserves to receive. If both are really desperate then they may expend more energy fighting that night than in having a bad day in the first place! 'Who had the worst day?' is an example of the competing pattern that we described earlier. Couples can often develop a unique sequence, which they dance over and over. It is what people do instead of getting their needs met directly and reasonably.

We call it the 'unfulfilment waltz', with pre-ordained moves for each partner. Like old time dancing, there is friction but no fulfilment! (Old time dancing is fascinating. A century or more ago, when people were supposedly chaste, faithful, and restrained in sexuality and when tables had covers on their legs, people used to dance by rubbing the fronts of their bodies together! It must have driven them up the wall! In recent decades, coinciding exactly with the promiscuous free-loving '60s, dancing became separate, expressive and disengaged. But enough of this digression.)

We invite you to take a minute here and figure out your and your partner's 'favourite' unfulfilment waltz, using the following short questionnaire. Once you have mapped the moves in this way, it all becomes clearer, and you'll find it quite impossible to repeat the mini-drama with the same intensity ever again. Which is great, for you can then move on to better things.

The steps in your unfulfilment waltz, or 'how you don't get what you want when you want it'
1 What is your most common thing you want, at present from your partner? (For example, time to listen, more touching, appreciation, breathing space, strong contact and reassurance, security, talking about the kids.)

_____

_____

2 What do you do when you feel this want (and your partner is around) instead of asking straight out? (For example, pick a fight, say how sick you are, complain about generalities, sulk, be martyrish, give _to_ them what you really want to receive _from_ them.)

_____

_____

_____

3 When you _do_ ask straight out, how do you sabotage it so that the person will be unlikely to respond well? (For example, are you sarcastic, do you ask demandingly or critically, or whiningly, make the demand too big, choose the wrong time?)

_____

_____

_____

4 How does your partner usually respond?

_____

_____

5 In what way do you counter-attack?

_____

_____

6 How does it usually end up? (For example, fight and reconciliation, fight and stand-off, just a stand-off, shrug it off but feel depressed, threats of a split up, sexual holding out at a later date, physical symptoms.)

_____

7 And lastly, for a good measure of aversion therapy, from which of your parents did you learn your side of this behaviour from?

Awareness and learning to ask

In writing this chapter, we were aware of the risk of giving you a serious self-diagnostic overload! You now know about your ratio of Parent, Adult and Child and whether your combination of personalities is rescuing, competing or disengaged. You know about needs collisions. You can recognise the moves in your unfulfilment waltz. Please don't let all this information take you down the easy slide from self-awareness to self-harassment! If you've made some new insights and connections, then congratulate yourself on your clarity and honesty, and get on to something better. The way to use self-knowledge is to accept the past, and be aware in the present. This has a double bonus. You can begin choosing to be different, and act from your intentions. But at the same time, your unconscious will make many changes with little effort by you. All you need to do is notice the things you do and say, without judging yourself.

We've found, over and over again, that when a couple (or parents and children) recognise the ways they *don't* ask for what they want, then it becomes increasingly obvious what to do. We have vocal chords, and a highly developed language ability, so that we can *ask* for what we want.

Asking with skill is a major life achievement. Janine, a friend of ours, sought marriage counselling. Her husband was suspicious and wouldn't go, so she went alone. The counsellor talked about many things with her, and sexual problems came up. Our friend told the counsellor that she hadn't really been satisfied for many years, that her man was doing things wrong by her. 'Then you must tell him!' said the counsellor. 'Be assertive!' End of session. Janine's husband was greeted that night with the news that he had been no good in bed for ten years. This was hardly helpful to the relationship. It was months before the man's hurt and anger diminished. All of this was so unnecessary. What is past is past, and must at some level have suited both partners to be that way, (and this is true of any past games or patterns that you may have been caught up in.) How much better if she had just said quietly at the right moment, 'Mmm, it'd feel even better if you just . . .'.

This is the form in which we would all prefer our feedback: *'You're doing fine, and would you like to know how to do really well?'*.

Human wants are not complicated unless you make them that way. Once you're fed and housed, most wants are psychological rather than practical. If you don't know what you want, try affection, time, talking, appreciation, rest, privacy, reassurance, safety, loving, variety and challenge, just to begin with!

Translating from feelings to wants

What if you still 'don't know what you want'? You may need some help with what is called 'emotional literacy' — how to read your own feelings. Emotions are the primary key to what is missing in your life at each moment. All mammals have four primary states:

Anger   tells you you're boxed in and need more freedom and space, or that you need people to take notice of you and stop ignoring your wants. Real anger should not be confused with defensiveness, which is really covered up fear.

Fear   tells you you're under threat and need some safety, protection, or information, or that a sensitive area has been touched upon.

Sadness   tells you that you're suffering loss or separation, and need to make contact. (If the loss is a permanent one, sadness flows into grief, and then it's a matter of experiencing the loss fully, going through it in order to go beyond it. Though some people try, it is harder to grieve alone.) Sadness can also be a gradual thing — a lack of appreciation by others, or the decline of self-esteem through lack of success. You need to be noticed and have your part recognised.

and for those who have forgotten . . .

Happiness tells you that you're doing something right, and to keep doing it!

This system is biological and present in every multi-celled animal. Even your goldfish has feelings. Feelings are a compass system designed to guide you moment by moment. As the human brain evolved into its present advanced form, higher functions like insight, speech and so on were grafted onto the emotional network, giving us almost literally an informed heart. Far from being irrelevant or fickle, your emotions also respond to your higher capacities like values and philosophies, as well as perceptions and intuitive messages. These many parts would overload you if they were directly accessed. Instead, as you weigh up a situation you 'get a feeling'. Nothing vague or hocus pocus, just a growing sense of 'I've had enough of this!' (anger), or 'I don't like this one bit!' (fear) or 'I don't know why, but gee this feels right!' (joy). It's a beautifully evolved system for integrating all your faculties, but emotions only work if you give them your attention, and you are honest with yourself about what you're feeling in the first place.

Emotional honesty isn't so hard

What do people mean by 'being honest with yourself'? Most people learn in childhood that some feelings are unacceptable, and others are more likely to lead to a successful outcome. They may learn to pretend one feeling on the outside, and deny another one that is happening deeper down. If, for instance, you get angry when you are threatened, this is usually not the core feeling. Fear is. So consider whether instead of lashing out, it might work better to voice your fear and seek reassurance.

If you get depressed (sad) when things don't work out, when events in your life are restricting you, this is probably not the core feeling. Anger often is. You may need to be more active. Speak up and let people know, instead of sulking.

If you get scared a lot, and rely on other people to help you out and reassure you constantly, maybe you need to get angrier sometimes and assert your own rights instead of letting others do it. (On the other hand, if you've got them so well trained, good luck to you!)

If you act happy all the time but aren't then stop pretending and figure out what you really want.

The above may take a little time to absorb. In intensive courses

we may spend six days with some very capable people, just helping them with the implications of the last few paragraphs. If you're ready for a change, though, then making the connections from emotions to wants is usually the place to start.

It's so simple, and yet makes such a huge difference. These two situations are so very similar, but worlds apart.

Situation One

Peter drives a truck all day. He comes home feeling lonely, but he doesn't admit this to himself in any clear way. He knows he is sick of his job. He knows he feels like a beer. He says something to his wife Cheryl, who says something back. The kids bicker and he yells at them, and she yells at him 'They'd be better if you spent more time with them, instead of watching the damned TV all night'. He feels strangely better, more alive, as he starts to yell at her. Sometimes when they fight like this, they also make up, later, when it's quiet, and make love. Sometimes though she goes cold, savage, and won't even speak. Though he wouldn't do it, at these times he sometimes wants to hit her, just to get her to react.

Situation two

Peter drives a truck all day. It's hard work but the money is good. He comes home and says hello to his wife, tells her it's good to see her. She comes over and gives him a squeeze. She tells the kids to quiet down, or go outside — they'll get time with Daddy later. She sits down for a drink with him, and they munch salami and crackers. Dinner can wait. The kids get noisy and bump the coffee table. He yells at them, good naturedly but loud, and they go into a bedroom to play. Peter and Cheryl sit for a few minutes more, not talking much, just enjoying the time. In a while she goes and makes tea, and he takes the kids outside. Later that night they talk more about things, concerns about this and that, and reassure each other, or make plans. She flirts a little, enjoying his response, glad she has a relaxed, practical man. It's early but they head for bed.

Sadness, anger, concerns, flow like a river. Dealt with smoothly, we can use these as a guide, always moving back towards balance and resolution, always trusting that needs can be met. Life can be dealt with, people can be reasonable, joy can be found.

Releasing your feelings

J. WRIGHT

In learning to track down your true self, there is no better ally than your own body. A growing number of therapists, usually called 'somatic' psychotherapists, now work with the body/mind interface. According to workers in this field, body sensations give direct and simple clues to what the mind is doing.

Anger is often stored in the shoulders and neck and head. When you learn to release it, you'll be angry with a kind of enjoyable feeling of strength, and with no further desire to hurt anyone else. You will just learn to take care of your own boundaries.

Sadness may be held back in the belly, or throat, or behind the eyes, and you may be prone to throat problems, sinusitis and hay-fever as a result. When you learn to release into sadness, you'll experience it as a beautiful fullness, which both cherishes what is lost and moves on to finding something new.

Fear is held in the chest, and sometimes the bowel. As you learn to experience and then release fear, you'll be scared very rarely, and when you are, you will use the fear as energy to rapidly get more safety and clarity in your life.

The above three feeling states, usually described by people as negative emotions, are better understood as 'imbalance' emotions. They tell you something is needed to restore the rightness. When you figure out what you really feel, it will ring true, and match your body sensations. You may not necessarily feel comfortable, but you *will* feel energised and literally 'moved' by the emotion. Sadness will wash through you like a waterfall. When you get angry it will feel righteous and strong, even fear will have an exhilarating quality to it. These different forms of arousal will direct your actions clearly and easily, and as you take action you will pass quickly on to a quieter, more harmonised and contented state.

Anger has but one purpose — to defend you and keep you free. Fear likewise, is the urge to be safe, to stay out of danger. Sadness is the capacity to let go of what is gone, and to be drawn to make deeper contact with what is. Freedom, safety, and contact are thus the elements of the fourth emotion, joy.

Once your emotions are in balance and able to flow freely, you will experience an easy continuum ranging from quiet contentment through to exhilaration and joy. It is normal, and natural, to expect to be joyful on a daily basis. People in western societies for a time accepted an extraordinary reduction in vitality and pleasure in exchange for the benefits of modern life, and we are only now beginning to regain what was lost. Owning, expressing, and dealing with, the so-called negative emotions, so long culturally repressed, leads to a more rapid resolution, and a return to joyfulness.

Finally, of the many forms which joy can take, the one central to the context of this book is the intense and outwardly focused form called love. Love as a sensation starts in the midline of your body near your heart. You will be aware of your eyes relaxing. Your pupils dilate and energy floods from the centre of your body up into your head, and down your arms and legs. Your heart rate increases moderately, there is a warm melting sensation overall, a softening of facial features and an all-pervasive sweet feeling. Love is a reaching out which has in it the anticipation of response from the loved one. There is an expectation of enfolding, sharing, openness and exchange.

Communicating your feelings to others

It's lunchtime. A young couple, office workers, sit together at an outdoor café. They have finished eating and it is time to move on, but they linger. An awkwardness creeps into their movements, as if something has been left unsaid. Finally it is the girl who shows the courage of the next step: 'I really like you . . . Can we have lunch again tomorrow?'.

He is looking back so intensely, smiling, almost forgetting to reply. 'Yeah!' They reach across and squeeze hands, before getting up to walk away together.

It's late evening. There is a banging of car doors in the street, and shouts of goodbye — a little high pitched and over-friendly. A couple wave briefly, then turn and walk back onto their own porch.

The man starts to speak, a little awkwardly. 'Love, thanks for trying to help in that argument. But I need to fight my own fights with Mum and Dad. Will you stay out of it next time?'

'But I was just wanting to back you up!'

'I know. I don't understand why, but it gets too complicated. I want to deal with them myself.'

'Okay. Suits me!'

'Thanks.'

The first stage in relating to others is a preparatory and inward step — reflecting to find out what you really do feel. The second is taking the risk, and developing the habit, of openness with other people — feeling easy and undefensive about sharing your reactions.

Ideally we should live out our lives in a web of comfortable and accepting relationships. Some cultures provide this but in western society we often appear to have lost the knack of just being real. The consequences of this are acute and widespread loneliness. Australian psychologist Bettina Arndt has pointed out how men, especially, will fail to emotionally support each other in times of acute need. She describes a farmer in middle-age, losing his farm to the banks after years of falling prices and drought. His neighbour, for decades a partner in work and life, comes to say goodbye, and can only stand awkwardly and mutter a few words of oblique comfort. It is a fact that words cannot change reality, but we can surely express things better than this — take the chance for comfort and healing. Strong caring feelings are present at these times (in fact the outwardly 'hard' men we have treated are often painfully sensitive to emotion). The failure is not of sensitivity, but of expression.

When positive feelings are not spoken or physically expressed, then how can they nourish? Again and again we meet this in our clients: people who *are* loved, and valued by their friends and families, but cannot feel sustained by this because it is never said out loud. The gap between the esteem people are held in, and the low self-esteem they suffer from, means that capable, loving and mature people (and the rest of us!) flounder needlessly in self-doubt.

Darren was a client of ours who sought help for crippling headaches and muscular pain. In groups he asked indirect questions about the meaning of violent fantasy and the need for control. We did not work directly with him for some time, wanting to establish the safety we sensed he needed. He became acutely uncomfortable when someone shed tears or expressed anger about long-ago events. We guessed that he had only ever been touched in a punishing way, and probably told how unworthy and useless he was while being hit or shaken. These two ideas were certainly deeply linked in his mind. We did not mention these ideas to him, but simply contradicted him whenever he was self-disparaging, and on one occasion invited group members to share their positive experiences of him. He reported two positive changes in the weeks that followed. He had started crying for no apparent reason, while lying with his wife in bed one night, and had experienced an enormous sense of relief from this. Secondly, he had yelled at his eight-year-old son who was misbehaving (something he never before allowed himself to do) and the child had been both co-operative and relaxed for most of the time since!

Having ignored the feeling level for so long, a person begins to sense the long-withheld energy, and can begin to believe that they will lose everything — their dignity, their control, even their sanity — if they 'open up'. In fact the opposite is true. Once we become at ease with this dimension, feelings can be acknowledged and dealt with without any great trauma. For men, especially, the news is clear. You can be courageous, protective and strong, and still fully experience your emotions. In fact it helps if you do.

Sometimes anger is the feeling that people are most reluctant to express. In many of our childhoods, anger was equated only with destructiveness and pain. However, much of the fighting between people who are in a relationship is an attempt to blow away barriers, to 'clear the decks' so that intimacy has a chance to grow. After all, when feelings are this intense they most likely reflect the high degree of investment and therefore of caring that exists, and which is unable to find more easy expression. All the words of a fighting couple (or a parent and adolescent yelling at each other), may just as well be translated as 'I love you, you so-and-so!'.

J.WRIGHT

Not only with those close to us, but even in superficial exchanges of life, you will find that honest talking, mixed with a good natured style, makes life exhilaratingly simple and real. 'Do you mind if I smoke?' 'Yes I do!' 'All right!' One very old woman we read of said 'When I was younger, I didn't care a lot for what other people thought. Now that I'm old, I don't give a damn!'

A necessary mask?

Where did the phoniness of such modern life come from, the empty phrases like 'Have a nice day' and 'Wonderful to see you'? Perhaps it is the sheer numbers of people we are exposed to in urban living. (Our Stone Age ancestors would meet perhaps 200 other human souls in the course of a whole lifetime.) Our sensory systems simply cannot cope with the overload. Remember Paul Hogan in *Crocodile Dundee* saying 'G'day' to each person in the Manhattan street, and then just giving up?

Perhaps you are aware of this yourself — the need to adopt a 'persona', a moderately cheerful, cynical, but above all conventional mask to present to the surge of people you have to deal with daily. It could hardly be otherwise.

Some kind of 'heart shielding' is necessary in our lives, but problems arise when some of us take this closedness into personal relationships where there should be the safety to be openhearted. The intimate social world of some people becomes as much an act as their office or social whirl persona. Husbands acting loving to their wives, and wives who won their husbands by pretending interest in their work or hobbies, pretending to laugh at their jokes, find the strain begins to show.

Almost all human behaviour can be understood as a need for contact, for mutual recognition. An artist strives to express his perceptions of life. A businessman wants to succeed so that he can 'show them!'. Our greatest hope in writing this book (the hope that sustains us through the years of toil!) is to achieve a feeling of connection with true experience, as if you the reader were looking us straight in the eye and saying 'Yes! That's it!'.

Connection is built simply by continually switching inwards, noting how we feel, and outwards, testing and trying out our reactions on others. Everything else flows from this: decisions about whether to be friends, to marry, to have children, to make changes. These things simply unfold from endless dialogue.

The results of emotional honesty affect everything. In everyday, trivial interactions with relative strangers we find we can be more spontaneous. In close relationships we find that we are safe enough, accepted enough, to journey deeper and deeper into the truth about ourselves.

What if all I feel is lousy?

Sometimes when people have been in miscommunication for a time, the surface feelings seem to be negative. If these negative feelings begin to be expressed as they happen, and both parties can let some of their feelings through in a measured way, without wanting to destroy or hurt the other, then things will soon begin to change and improve. Be careful, though, to be honest with yourself before you are honest with them. When you feel a wish to hurt another person emotionally or physically, acknowledge that this is just a wish to have them respond to you, to prove they care. Find a better way to get this response.

You may have someone in mind right now that you would like to be more honest with, and therefore closer to. If you find this hard to do, remember that the key is to state your emotions, but not to indulge in emotionality. Think about this difference. If what you really want to do is cash in accumulated bad feelings, or to get revenge, to hurt, then the outcome will be no surprise to you! If your heartfelt goal is to remove the obstacles to closeness, to make the changes in them and you that will re-admit love, then you'll be rewarded. You will know the difference.

A patient of ours tells her story:

> For years I felt aggrieved and vengeful. Although we stayed together, he continued to see other women. When we argued, we could both be very destructive and horrible. When he finally sought help, he came to me afterwards and said that he felt he had been at fault. I had an urge to say 'Yes, you were' and to pour out a litany of long-held examples to prove it. Strangely I felt no anger towards him, only anger at the wasted years that we had spent in bitterness. I found myself saying that neither of us were at fault, that we had a lot going for us, and that we could use this determination to change things. I guess I surprised myself.

A lot of fights can be seen as the desire to have an impact on the other person, and so to prove that they care. Many people grew up in families where they were not noticed unless there was a problem, and the only intense contact was through hitting and punishment. Adults from this kind of background often experience positive strokes as unfamiliar, and not believeable. A rousing fight, although destructive and even violent, makes these people feel connected, real and noticed.

Everyone knows at least one couple who have been together for years and years and have fought their way through each and every day of that time. If they were to win a luxury holiday they would argue about when to take it, and where to go, and would accuse each other of 'spoiling it all' when they got back. Just notice however, with couples who fit this description, how fit they are for their age, and despite their apparently unsatisfying life, and how if their partner isn't around they miss them and arrange to fight with someone else!

If you've become hooked on the intensity of negative relationships, then practice is needed to intensify the positive, if you are to thrive. Here is an exercise in developing this capacity.

> Arrange a time to sit together and talk and be uninterrupted. Arrange this properly — phone off the hook, children asleep, a good meal inside you. Talk about what you are enjoying about your life right now, and what is the next step for you. Where do you want to be headed? What do you want to achieve, and what do you want to develop in your life at the moment? As one partner does the above, the other listens, and helps to clarify exactly how you feel, think, and what you want, without digressing or reacting otherwise. If you are the listening partner, keep your focus on the idea of your partner being totally and completely fulfilled and happy, and how that would be for them and you. After fully doing this, reverse roles and it is your turn to explore and detail what makes and will make you most happy.

Conflict as a Path to Intimacy

Conflict is life. A long time ago, some rocks rubbed up against each other, lightning struck, water bubbled, and it all began on schedule. Life started with friction and has been friction ever since. But some friction can be beautiful!

As long as you live, you will experience conflict at every turn of the road. Your wishes and those of others will appear to be at odds. But staying with — and working through — the conflict gives results much better than just getting your way. This is the paradox of human relations. To paraphrase the Rolling Stones' song, you can't always get what you want—life has much better plans for you than that. We'll explore next the two poles of the conflict spectrum: full-on fighting, which has a special role in close relationships, and the quieter negotiation process called 'the no-compromise route to fulfilment'.

Why do couples fight?

Usually long before they have children, and certainly after they do, most couples discover that in some areas they don't get on. Not a constant negativity, but occasionally and around certain issues in your life, an unmistakeable energy build up. This is usually an indicator of the need for a fight. There may be couples who are exceptions to this rule, but we have never met any! *We don't know anyone anywhere, in any relationship, who doesn't sometimes need to fight.* We suspect that if you don't fight with your partner at least occasionally, you are either too frightened, or you enjoy misery, or you just don't care.

Having started on a provocative subject in a provocative way, let us define our terms. Fighting is the rapid, noisy, expulsion of feelings and information about *difference*. It stands out from normal communication because of its intensity, and in its dual

function, which is both to break down barriers that have come about inadvertently between people, and to send through a message that (because of these barriers) has not previously been heard. Often the message itself is very positive. Even when the content is 'You don't understand me, you're not taking account of my needs', the reason you are saying these things is because you want there to be understanding, and you think the relationship is worth fighting for. Sometimes you have to kick someone's door open to hand them a flower!

What do we mean by difference? No two people are identical, and so no two people can possibly get on well all the time. Difference creates a spark, it makes life interesting and vital, and is the essence of relationships. If you are different from someone you have no involvement with, there is no need to fight. It's when you are involved and care that the fighting is necessary. The combination of difference plus closeness creates energy flow. Small energy flows are called discussion, stimulation, give and take, and big ones are called fighting. Fights can easily be destructive, so it's vital that you learn to fight safely and well. But fight you must.

Beyond the honeymoon phase

People often process differences in the same way they process the household garbage: you can take it out often, every time a little accumulates, or you can get really junked up and then have a big clean out. You can either have little fights, sorting things out often, or wait and have a really big one. One counsellor friend of ours has noted that most divorces are not over big things. He says 'It's usually five thousand dirty teaspoons that destroy a marriage!'.

Speaking personally, we prefer big fights, and are most happy when living on a few hectares where we can be noisy without alarming the neighbours.

A couple doesn't usually start out fighting. In simple terms, the 'honeymoon phase', during which you adore everything about the other person, passes into the 'clash phase', where you begin to learn what to do with your differences. The solving of fights — the ability to disagree, yet maintain respect for the other, and to figure out something that is not just a backdown — is what makes the difference between infatuated newlyweds and a real relationship.

You don't know someone, and you certainly can't be safe with someone, until you both know you can fight safe and fair.

A young couple with whom we worked described to us how they learned to fight fair. We were very impressed with their good sense. Drew and Erica had been living together for three years, a relationship that, in their words, 'just sort of grew step by step'. Permanence wasn't really discussed, they were just going along from day to day. Gradually, though, things started becoming more tense between them, they found each other's company less satisfying. Nothing seemed to be quite right, and yet nothing big was wrong. Also Erica began to suffer from recurring illnesses. Talking things over it occurred to them both that they never fought, and that they would in fact find it very hard to fight. There was a magazine article Erica had read saying couples should fight to clear the air. Why didn't they do it? In Drew's family no-one had ever fought. In his whole childhood he could remember only two incidents that could be called blow ups, and at those times, people took off without explanation. They simply went away for what to a child seemed like ages, but in fact was only a few hours. Drew recalled finding it a horrible experience. Erica's childhood had been quite the opposite. In her family people had fought all the time, and brooding silences alternated with violent outbursts, of which she and her sisters and brothers were often the recipients.

So both Drew and Erica had these semi-conscious fears still current in their lives. As Drew explained, 'If we fought, my nightmare was a walk-out abandonment. Hers was being hit and hurt, and never feeling safe with me again.' It was a deadlock, but a remedy suggested itself. The couple arrived at an agreement — a specific, spoken contract that neither would walk out of the house in a fight, and neither would touch the other while a fight was taking place. To cap it off, they promised to stay together for the next six months, whatever happened. The pair spoke these contracts out loud to each other, sitting face-to-face in what must have been a rather moving moment. This was the first time they had made a commitment of any kind in their friendship. Six months seemed an awfully long time. From a generation and a sub-culture that rejected marriage as largely a farce, they were re-inventing the concept of commitment, and making it real for themselves.

The result at first was anti-climactic. In Erica's words, 'We just suddenly felt very tired, but happy, and went to bed'. The next day though, something happened. One of the pair exclaimed something with a little more force than usual, the other partner snapped back, and it was on! Drew recalls 'I could not believe the force and volume of my own words, like a hurricane coming out of my mouth, and I was shaking, but somehow knew where the edge was. I went to open a door, which was loose on its hinges (in an old, rented house), it balked, and I just pulled the whole door free, and slammed it down on a table. The whole time, part of me was watching myself, amazed, bemused, but still in control, keeping to the rules!'

Erica felt very scared, but mostly angry, and stayed there, yelling at Drew, saying a lot of honest and interesting things, and the energy seemed to peak and then all just sort of petered out into gasping, and laughter, and passion, and, well . . . we'll leave them there.

Making it safe to fight

Fighting needs primarily to be *safe*. Whatever your fears, they need to be dealt with *before* you can begin to fight. The issues for Drew and Erica were the two universal nightmares: fear of abandonment and fear of violence. From childhood, we may have learned to experience these as life-threatening (which for a small child they are). You may well have one or both of these fears in your own repertoire, and perhaps some specific fears of your own, all of which can be talked about and dealt with through reassurance and commitment. Once these are excluded as possibilities (through mutual contracting), then fighting becomes just so much noise — the expression of feeling, and the assertion that *I matter*. Contracts can be as short term as needed to be realistic and trustworthy — a week, a month, a year. You can contract about sexual fidelity, about violence, about motor vehicle safety, about who is home when, about how long you will promise to stay in the partnership and so on, *if the need exists* (by which we mean, if either partner feels unsafe about the other's behaviour). Don't contract for something you can't/won't fulfil. If someone breaks a contract, then this means that they promised too much. Don't accept such a contract a second time, unless it is somehow modified to cover the reasons for failing the first time. If someone breaks a contract three times, then they are lying to you. What are you doing in a relationship like that?

The traditional marriage contract has failed in that it promises too much, and therefore no-one believes it. 'Until death do us part' sounds awfully like a jail sentence! One day you may be able to say this in truth. Until then it's better to only promise what you know you can fulfil.

Have a look at the movie, available on video, called *Man Woman and Child*, based on the book by Eric Segal. In this excellent film there is a full-on yelling and screaming fight which is nonetheless totally safe and vastly constructive. Since by this stage in the plot the couple have had three unsuccessful attempts to air their differences, the audience has been known to applaud the fighting! For those of us brought up on constraint, it is an exhilarating experience. For those brought up on aggression, it is paradoxically very reassuring to watch.

What about the children?

Since you need to fight, it's better to fight in front of children than in secret. This is simply because they know anyhow when a fight is going on, or has gone on. If you attempt to conceal your fights, then this adds to their fear. The message they receive is 'Our fights are so dangerous, or at least so shameful, that they have to be hidden'. Tell your children that you need to let out some feelings, that nobody will leave or be hurt and that nobody is being put down. Remind them that they too often get angry and yell, and it doesn't last long. With older children you can put out a 'storm warning' so they can choose to go off and be out of the firing line. They fight sometimes and so do you, and it's no big deal.

It's not harmful to fight in front of the children, unless the way you fight is something to be ashamed of. You can be loud, expressive, angry, and immediate, without being destructive or hurtful. But only say and do what you are proud of. If you reflect back on fights that caused you some shame, it will most likely be that destructive things were said or done at these times.

The kind of fighting which we endorse need have no put downs or recriminations. Simply say '*I feel* ____ *when you* ____ *and I want* ____*.!*' The aim is that, when a fight is over, you have no regrets, but can honestly feel 'I said what I meant, and I meant what I said. And it's over now and it's fixed!'.

Children will always find fighting between adults somewhat

uncomfortable, but much, much better than brooding silences. Awareness of the kids' needs will prevent you from being self-indulgent with your anger, and keep you to the real thing.

How much to involve kids in disagreements is an important question, and needs delineating. We believe that in small arguments — the majority — kids need to be told 'We are working this out, don't interrupt, it's not your problem'. If a child intrudes in an argument to help, then *both* parents must tell them that the fight is not to do with them, and that it will be worked out in a good way. Serious, longer term arguments about issues like jobs, houses and marriage break-ups, should be dealt with at time set aside from the children. They are not the proper concern of children, until the adult situation has been resolved (at which stage they may be consulted). Sudden outbursts about serious issues, with the children present and clearly distressed, must be avoided. We've all done it, and learnt not to.

Rules to fight by

All fights have rules and rituals. Think of children fighting in the school playground. There is an elaborate sequence of name calling, eliciting the support of friends, jaw jutting and lip pouting, chest pushing and finally (if all else fails) a very few flailed punches, and someone is crying or the teachers come, and it's all over. The rules are inviolate, differ for girls and boys and vary from place to place. The result is that with hundreds of children over thousands of hours, real injuries are as rare as hen's teeth. Among adults too, fighting is never really an out of control or unpredictable phenomenon: even in violent and seemingly chaotic families, it follows rules. The trick is to find those rules which help you to arrive at a ritual in your own couple or family, which enhances problem solving, closeness, and personal growth.

Here are the best suggestions we have found so far, given to us by our teachers Ken and Elizabeth Mellor:

1 **Stay on the goal** Remember what you are fighting for and about. Don't veer off into last year . . ., your mother . . ., on our wedding day . . .! Keep all fighting goal-directed — focused on what it is you really want to resolve.

2 Never be abusive This is central. Whenever you use a derogatory name or description of another human being, you program them towards being what you describe. What you call them, they progressively become. Abuse is verbal violence — it destroys personality.

You can be angry, expressive and impactful without ever being destructive. Stick to 'I feel ____ when you ____', and make noise, elaborate, list and detail, but don't name-call. If your reaction to this is 'But I can't help it, it just comes out', our response is 'you're lying'. It's your mouth, and you control what comes out of it.

3 Stay present and stay temporary Make all your statements in the here-and-now: 'Right now I feel like I never want to see you again!'; 'Right now I hate you!'. Remember how children process fighting. They make these absolute, vehement statements, and moments later are reconciled. Children know the secret. What you let out, passes.

4 Have time-out signals Sometimes the fight becomes too much — tiring, or scarey, or overwhelming, or practically ill-timed. Have a pre-arranged signal which either person can give which calls an automatic halt. (One couple we know invented a 'stop' hat, which was always on the hall stand and either could go and put on. It sounds quaint, but it worked.) Stopping the fight has interesting results. You are left hanging, certainly, but in the time that ensues you begin to clarify what is just your own 'junk', and what real issues remain. You return to continue the fight later if need be, but things will have subtly changed. Often, if you're honest, you'll have noticed yourself losing the heat of the hate and anger (say while away at work for the day), but then struggling to revive it as you come home, as if you feel you can't let them off that easy!

Feelings (unlike contracts and commitments) are fickle and inconsistent, so don't try to hold them frozen. 'I hate you/I love you' is a very normal feeling between lovers.

5 Do something enjoyable mid-fight When you've broken off from the struggle as suggested in 4 above, find an activity that is normally enjoyable for you to do alone — anything from going to a movie to eating a block of chocolate to having a swim at the beach. It may be a little hard to begin since you will not be 'in the mood', but that's the whole point. Pleasurable activity crossed over with your fighting feelings will help to more rapidly tease out the parts which are over with, the parts which are your own issues and not your partner's, and the parts which you are genuinely wanting to change in them.

6 Don't compromise yourself, but do be flexible Sometimes your feelings change, and you can give and take. At other times, you will find that you must hold to your views — not out of pride, but because to do otherwise would be untrue to yourself. Compromising yourself always rebounds — you feel resentful, and are likely to save up your bad feelings for an equaliser! Better to fight for a year about something that matters, and find true acceptance and reconciliation at the end of it, than to fake it for an uneasy peace.

7 Accept the present and forget the past The past is over and cannot be changed. You may need to tell your feelings about the past, *once*, but then move on to fixing now.

'You did that at Dad's funeral. You fussed about my tie then, and I hated that. It was the last thing I needed.'
'But you were . . .'
'I just want to tell you that wasn't what I needed!'
'Okay . . . How about now?'
'I'd like a hug . . .'

Always return to the present. It's the only time that matters.

8 Remember that the aim of all fighting is closeness Fighting in an intimate relationship is solely aimed at clearing the decks, removing rubbish that has cluttered the free flow of energy and experience. Fighting right will leave only love when it is over.

The approach we take to fighting is a dramatic reversal of old assumptions held by many people ('I couldn't help myself'; 'He made me do it'). Fighting is a choice you make, with a goal of getting closer. It can be emotional, without being destructive. You *can* be angry, and still be master of yourself.

There is no doubt that this takes skill, maturity, and effort. Few people in close relationships have not felt the terror that comes from a suddenly escalating miscommunication. Some small difference suddenly taps into deeper conflicts that have grown unnoticed, and suddenly things seem to be out of control. One's whole life's efforts — children, home, career, and intimate relationship — suddenly seem about to be broken in pieces.

It's precisely because of this intensity — the huge investment we make in loving another person — that we must learn to fight properly. There is no need to take chances. Establish what relationship contracts you need to be safe with another person — before you start fighting. Don't be afraid early in a relationship to ask for monogamy, for commitment, if only for a limited time to begin with. Make all fights transitory. Leave long-term decisions and changes to calmer times. Leave childishness behind and learn to deal and fight with the constructive passion that adult relationships deserve.

The 'No-Compromise' Route to Fulfilment

Fighting is for accumulated, high energy differences. But sometimes you are aware of large or small issues which don't cause anger, just require some help to resolve. This particularly comes into play when discussing the future. Often in our own marriage we have had great difficulty in making long-term plans, or to be more honest, we just didn't! It was hard to know what we wanted, and the present was always fairly engrossing. But the things that come from long-term plans — special holidays, a different job, a nice house — tend to not happen if not planned for.

Finding agreement on goals

One reason for not planning is that you might disagree. What if (as couples often find) you love each other deeply, but have very different goals in life? What if your wants and needs are in conflict? Should you meet half way? Should one of you back down? The answer is 'Neither'. Wants and needs unfold in a streamlike way. They tend simply to reflect our present moment, where we are at right now, rather than any long term direction. For example:

'Gee I'm sick of being cold. A holiday in the tropics would be great.' ('Or maybe I should turn the heater on!')

'I want to quit this job, sell the house, get divorced, and live on a houseboat.' ('Or maybe I need a weekend camping!')

Wants and needs are transitory, but they are also the only guidance system we can rely on to truly reflect our nature. Therefore we must express them, and move towards them, without prejudicing the future. The way to get your needs actually 100 per cent met is to go for them, *but only one step at a time.*

Ian wants to own a nice house with a garden, to actually be able to put down roots and know he will stay put, while his wife Jan wants to go on a world trip, to see something of life before it's too late (whatever that means). If Jan was to back down, right now, to Ian's wishes, then years later she would still dream of the trip she sacrificed, and resent Ian for 'stopping her' having it. Likewise if Ian went with her on the trip, then he may count every dollar spent on the journey, make Jan miserable, and years later scan the papers and tell her about houses they could have afforded, and so on. Yuk!

What the couple *can* do, is to *take small steps in the direction of their wishes* honestly and openly, maintaining communication. Jan can get brochures and prices and let Ian look at them without commitment. Ian can look at houses, with Jan going along with an open mind. Through all this, both will be aware of how their needs and wishes actually move and change. We won't predict the outcome, but if a couple have part of their interest and investment in each other, then *things will work out.*

Jan may go alone for a shorter trip. Ian may decide to go too, or he might stay behind. Ian may pay for the house himself, with Jan making a smaller contribution. Jan may have fun thinking about trips, but discover a growing wish to have a baby (with any luck Ian's). They may eventually both go on a small trip and buy a small house — so that the outcome is a compromise, even though the route to it was not. Jan may be surprised to find that once she feels free to take the trip, that she actually wants a house, but Ian conversely decides he wants to go round the world, and they have to start all over again! Or they may realise they're good friends but not compatible partners, and separate. If this is right, it's right! This process is the stuff of life, and getting there is not half but all the fun. This kind of approach isn't easy for people who like to have things all mapped out. But life isn't mapped out. You don't grow a tree by placing a branch there, and a leaf there, and working to a plan. You plant and water and shelter a tree, and it grows in a way that is its own. Relationships have this quality too. Some trust in the future is needed, or there would be no trees.

Life in a family or couple becomes easier when you realise that long-term plans are fine, as long as you can vary them with circumstance. One of the primary circumstances will be your partner's needs and wishes, and these too will change. But so will yours! The secret is not to definitely make a commitment to action, at any one stage, until it really is the moment to make a move, and to be open and honest about your wishes, rather than locked in out of spite, all the way along. This is the 'no-compromise' route to fulfilment. Somehow, when people do this, what one wants fits with what the other wants, in a mutually satisfying way. The way to get your needs actually met 100 per cent is to go after them, *but only one step at a time . . .*

How much do you want it?

Let's take a simpler example. In smaller day-to-day decisions, we devised our own way of getting a solution to apparent conflict. Say, for instance, that Steve wants to spend a day walking on the mountain near where we live, with Shaaron coming too. The old 'man, mountain and faithful woman' fantasy! Shaaron wants to visit her family two hours away in Launceston, and doesn't want to go along.

> **Shaaron:** How much do you want to go walking on the mountain?
>
> **Steve:** About 70 per cent. How much do you want to go to Launceston?
>
> **Shaaron:** 85 per cent.
>
> **Steve:** (with a wry grin) Okay. Let's go to Launceston!

Steve may end up climbing a Launceston mountain, or he may not. Who knows what he will feel like by then? The catch with this method, as you'll already have noted, is that you have to be honest, or else it's just an auction, but it will usually work out

fair in the long run, without you having to keep a balance sheet. Your feelings and needs do have a definable strength from moment to moment. Pigheadedness interferes for a while, but that's no fun.

Of course there are games people can play instead of being honest. Eric Berne in *Games People Play* catalogued many of these with delightfully explicit names: 'If it weren't for him'; 'Look what you made me do'; 'Now I've got you, you sonofabitch' and so on. Men and women often play a game around safety and bravery (freedom and restriction).

When we lived by the water, Steve would sometimes look out to sea, and decide to take the rowboat out, though there were whitecaps visible from the house. He wouldn't just do it though. That would be too simple. He would tell Shaaron of his plans, in a slightly adolescent voice. She would then, according to the plan, tell him it was too rough. He would argue, she would insist, and he would stay indoors. And sulk. Not a bad case, but sulk nonetheless.

Shaaron doesn't fall for things too often. Next time he tried it on (another windy weekend), she said, 'Okay, whatever you like'. He was caught off balance.

'It is kind of rough out there . . .' ('Stop me!').

'Oh, you'll be okay . . . I'll come and watch.'

Minutes later, he is standing in chest-high icy water, battling a small rowboat and unable to even get beyond the shore break. He gets cold, bruised and wet, while Shaaron watches from the shore.

'It's too rough', Steve explains rather obviously as he drags the boat back across the sand. Shaaron just smiles sweetly.

Remember that You're Twins

The idea that 'you marry your twin', introduced in the last chapter, is especially valuable in solving and moving beyond recurrent communication difficulties. It may be that if you have trouble with an aspect of your partner's make-up, then this may reflect your difficulty with this same trait, unacknowledged, in yourself.

A friend of ours called Peter wrote to us about how this principal freed him and his partner Sheila from arguments on a very common source of disagreement — money.

> I find that if I get into a blaming mood, attributing certain qualities to Sheila, say spending too much, being untidy, or whatever, these are always equally true of me! I have really tried (believe me!) and cannot find anything to blame in Sheila which isn't true at some level

for me too. Sheila once bought an ancient 30 foot Huon Pine whaleboat for the kids to play on in the backyard! I agreed to this but grumbled about it whenever I needed some excuse to grumble. Then *she* found *my* computer software invoices! Another example: I tease *her* for not exercising enough and not being healthy, the next day *I* get the flu! Every argument I start to indulge in falls apart as I see how I'm the same. I don't feel bad about it, just real. It kind of stops you in your tracks. If we decide to save money, we both can do it. If we decide to have a clean beautiful house, we both do it. If I arrogantly want to get Sheila's act together in some dimension of our life, I no longer hassle her. I just get my part of it together, and her part seems to flow along as well. It's very strange!

To change them, change yourself

You can get your partner to change, but only by changing yourself. A wife complains to a counsellor about her husband's lack of interest. Given the chance to talk to him in the counselling room, she can only rattle on about what is wrong, she is no longer (if ever) able to converse in a positive, interested way. After some discussion, she realises that she also is unavailable. If he were to change, she would not know what to do about it. With this insight, she begins to learn the pleasure and rewards of casual, ongoing contact, and finds her partner happy to reciprocate.

If you want to test our role complementarity in your own marriage or relationship, choose some way in which you take a role that is different from your partner. One common issue would be money. For instance, often one partner is cautious, while the other is 'free spending'. If you are the cautious one try a little experiment — go on a (moderate!) spending spree. If you are the one who spends freely, try being ultracareful, and encouraging your partner to be even more careful than usual. The results will fascinate you!

The reversing of roles is a part of smooth growth of a couple. At our house when we are very relaxed and having some days off, our son will start to call either of us Mummy or Daddy interchangeably. We correct him, but find the phenomenon interesting. As couples start to develop and change, and as communication and self-esteem grow, they will often discover reversals of old patterns that are unsettling to begin with, but eventually a source of great freedom. This often happens with physical health and energy levels. One partner may have been the energetic one, the other one tending to be weak and lethargic. As the latter chooses to be healthy, the other partner becomes uncharacteristically sleepy!

Often a 'hyperactive' partner (i.e. a workaholic) has a depressed spouse. We believe that couples exchange energy in such a way that one can be the 'battery' which the other draws on. When the 'depressed' spouse claims back this energy, the previously over-active, agitated partner runs out of steam. Again this is just a step on the road to health. Both eventually become masters of their own vitality levels. Remember the letter from our client, quoted earlier in this chapter, where the couple changed almost every aspect of their lives in order to overcome what seemed to be the wife's health problem? We are curious as to how many 'workaholics' depend in some way on the energy of others, and thus are maintained in an unbalanced lifestyle which, like the stock market, would benefit from an occasional 'correction'.

Twins know what the other is doing

As part of the twinness of partners, it is rarely possible to have secrets between couples of long-standing. We may play a game of one deceiving, the other being deceived, but there is a level at which each one always knows what the other is doing and thinking. There is, for instance, no such thing as a secret 'affair'. The invasion of a couple's bond is such that both partners know instantaneously when this takes place, though many choose to ignore it.

Some couples of long standing report experiences which can only be described as telepathic — a clear and accurate knowledge of the other's thoughts, actions or needs. For many other people, there is just a vague sense of connection with fleeting moments of lucid communication, which are probably put down to coincidence.

When couples split up, it may be that the twinness has been outgrown — that the similarity (especially in terms of impairment!) which drew the people together, and deepened their connection for a while, was diminished as they grew more whole. As well as the angry, bitter kind of separations which are often portrayed in the media, many 'real life' people just quietly become different,

so that it grows hard to imagine them ever having been close in the first place. Once upon a time, we used to get distressed about how 'bloody' some break-ups could be, but now believe there is such a thing as a necessary slashing free to get rid of long accumulated 'stuckness'. It's as if years of over-adapting to the other person needs to be vigorously spat out! Knowing this makes it easier for friends and family to support both parties, avoid taking sides, and wait for a separated peace to return.

In time, all couples are 'broken up' through death. We have begun to wonder if, between couples who have achieved full openness over decades of time, there is any need for grief or loss when one partner eventually dies. We have noticed that grief is often most painful when communication is incomplete, or there is unfinished business that has prevented total trust. It may be that in some couples towards the end of their lives, the awareness of the other is now so complete that their physical ending is not a loss at all. It's a nice thought, and if it can be thought, perhaps it can be done.

CHAPTER 4

Then Along Come the Kids

She: Then there's Angie. She's so damned
        independent for a six-year-old. She's wilful
        and defiant. She won't do anything without
        arguing every little detail. I talk to her till
        I'm blue in the face.

We: Sounds like a very intelligent child!

She: Oh, yes . . . She is that.

We: Who does she remind you of?

She: Huh?

We: In your whole life, who do you know like
        her?

She: Huh? . . . Oh! (she smiles and sighs in the
        same movement) Well, it's obvious isn't it?

We: What's obvious?

She: Me. She's just like me!

How Your Children Will Grow You Up

Your couple relationship is going along fine. Things are falling
into place, you're beginning to understand and be comfortable with
your partner, and then what happens? Little persons begin to arrive
on the scene. Kapoww!

J. WRIGHT

There are books without number on the topic of raising children, but they almost all miss the central point — that care of children flows from the care of parents. You can't discuss children without discussing parents, and it is only through parental self-awareness that the puzzles of childrearing finally make sense. The key to living with children is knowing that this role requires nothing less than a complete overhaul of your own personality.

The most honestly selfish reason why we have kids, and the reason for the extraordinary satisfaction that parenthood gives, is that it deepens and reworks our own development more than any other experience can. The love of another adult is a transformative experience, but the practical giving of love to children is what really purifies you in the fire! In short, your children will bring you up!

The process starts from conception. Let us illustrate this from our own experience. Every parent-to-be experiences a desire for things to be perfect, and we were no exception. Our work had made this even more the case. Shaaron had been a nurse, and worked in a number of different hospitals. Both of us had worked treating families where parent/child bonding was a problem, which had not been helped by the hospital practices of the day. We felt that although hospitals were improving they were still places for the sick, or for people who had been conditioned to rely totally on external support, and were not the environment for such a normal and personal event as the birth of a healthy baby. Therefore we embarked on the most highly planned homebirth in history! When the due date approached, we had ready on call two fine midwives (one a family member and one a friend), plus a doctor willing to call over if need be, plus all the joyful paraphernalia one needs at a birth. One morning Shaaron's 'waters' broke with a Niagara Falls gush, and the real adventure began.

Thirty-six hours later, despite a strong, pleasurably proceeding labour, and a healthy heartbeat from within, our infant-to-be showed no signs of emerging. Our midwives both concurred that we should transfer to hospital. Since it was this kind of judgement that we had chosen them for, we sadly packed our things. The overall feeling was of being powerless, and yet not quite defeated. We were surrendering but not submitting, since it was destiny that we were having to go along with. The next morning, baby Rohan was delivered by epidural Caesarian, with Steve alongside ready to take and hold him, in an environment of machines and strangers which had now become necessary. We were satisfied, both with our early choices, and our flexibility in the face of circumstance. There had been enormous emotional demands in having to 'hand over', surrendering our precious privacy and control, and moments of intense sadness and fear for both of us. (One altercation with an unbelievably rude nurse actually helped us to regain strength, and some phone calls to close friends seemed to clear the emotional decks as we went along.) A baby was born. The biggest negative was Shaaron being postoperatively laid up, instead of an active new mother as planned, but we made up for that. It was the hardest day of our lives so far, and yet it was great! We will certainly go for a home delivery next time, which our research tells us is a very reasonable chance.

The reason we've mentioned our experiences here is that it gave us a very clear message, our first practical understanding of what being a parent means. You have to make plans and aim for your ideals, but at the same time you must know that life will decide, each step of the way, what actually unfolds. By adapting to this, and yet continuing to work for what you want, you will be victorious.

And that was only the beginning! We're sure you'll agree, if you've been there, that the experience of parenthood is *a meeting with yourself*.

This chapter will detail some of the ages, stages and issues that parenthood will bring to the surface. First though, we'll explore the concept of recycling which helps in understanding and navigating these stages.

Recycling? Isn't that about cans?

You are never completely *un*prepared for parenthood. Your childhood has made you expert in at least one form of parenting — your own parents' way of doing it. For a couple of decades you have unconsciously 'videotaped' their every move, and expression, every raised eyebrow and heartfelt sigh. This is now stored, just below the level of awareness in your grey matter 'memory banks'. The tapes sit there gathering dust, and waiting for someone to press the button and play them again: Mum and Dads' Greatest Hits!

One of the commonest reasons people give for coming to our parenting workshops is 'I don't want to pass my hang-ups on to my kids. I don't want them to feel like I did'. We take time to put people at ease in this respect. You simply cannot make it as hard for your kids as it was made for you. Each generation makes very substantial progress over the last (and each generation still passes on some imperfections). You simply (!) do the best you can.

Unconscious parenting

It's normal to find that between the ideals of the young couple (or single parent), and actual day-to-day matters of parenting, there is a strange gap: *things often don't work out as they are planned*. This is not because our goals are unreal or idealistic, but because of the simple fact — *that most parenting is not conscious*. While we work hard at saying what we really want to say to our children, doing what we believe is right, trying to apply what friends suggest or we've read in books, the fact is that we are constantly reacting to unconscious internal needs that we barely understand. It's as if unconscious urges flow across conscious intentions, leaving little eddies and ripples on the surface of our lives. We struggle to be our true selves, but find that sometimes very contradictory messages are coming through.

Fortunately, children are mentally robust, and can live with a little ambiguity. As our friend, therapist and youthworker Susan Lane puts it, 'You'd have to work really hard to screw up a kid'. Confused family communication was once thought by some to be the cause of schizophrenia, but therapists investigating this found that *all* families give confusing messages quite a lot of the time. (This doesn't mean that we shouldn't strive to be as conscious, and straight-talking, as we possible can. If we eliminated the craziness of ordinary life, we would also empty the waiting rooms of psychiatrists.)

Caring about your children makes you want to get yourself 'right'. But clearing your body and mind of old confusions and hang-ups is a lifelong process, in which we are all mid-stream. In each generation we make things a little clearer, and our kids will continue the process with their offspring. (What good psychotherapy is all about is speeding up this process — saving a generation or two of confusion.)

From the above, you'll begin to realise that something as 'everyday' as raising children (if you stay open to what it will teach you) can be the ultimate training in self-awareness. The challenge is intensified because your children are so close to you, and such an accurate reflection of your own vulnerability, and therefore so good at taking you right to the limit of your abilities! The joint project of raising your children while raising yourself, while also (if you're in a couple) relating intimately to another adult on a very similar journey may sound daunting! Fortunately there is a simple, demystifying principle which underlies most of what goes on between the generations. This is the concept of recycling.

So that's why I sometimes feel young

Every parent knows that children grow through stages. Newborns are in an absorbing and passive stage, where the main issues are safety and closeness. Two-year-olds are learning to deal with a world that sometimes says no, and so on. But what if these stages are not completely successful, has a person 'missed out'? The answer is no. At about age twelve, the same issues from birth to preadolescence are re-run for a second time. Safety, exploratoriness, learning to think, socialising, and independence each in their turn become issues again. Adolescence is literally a second childhood. Even then, many of these lessons are not learned completely. Therefore as an adult, life will continue to restimulate learning that is primarily childhood related. Parenthood brings the sequence into sharp focus yet again, so that in a sense being a parent is a third childhood! The stages your child is passing through will either have been resolved by you already, or will be drawn to your attention continually until you resolve them for yourself, and can thus help your child too. In the pages that follow we'll provide many examples of how this happens, and how to use this awareness.

Do you experience times in family life when you lose your normal clarity, and feel confused, out of control, or ineffective? It's a fairly safe prediction that this is being caused by recycling of your own childhood. From the moment one even thinks about becoming a parent, the events of one's own childhood begin to be evoked. We are suddenly dealing not just with our planned new family, but with the historical child in ourselves at the same time. Beneath the surface of intentionality, deep currents move.

Here's a specific example of recycling from some friends of ours. Ian and Julie are young therapists who trained with us, and have some advantages in knowing what to do. They put this knowledge to good practice. Ian takes up the story:

> For a long time in our relationship, Julie and I did not feel ready to have kids. Over a ten year period, we became masters of the demanding business of contraception and fertility control! When we knew we were ready to start a family, we went ahead and conceived with special delight. So far so good. As Julie's belly swelled up, and we began to make plans for the birth (still five or six months away), I found a frequent sense of unease coming over me, which I could not easily pin down. Over a few days, I grew more clearly frightened. We discussed it, and at Julie's invitation I did some searching into the images and half-conscious associations in my mind. (It helps to be in the business.) Sure enough, when I thought about the coming birth, and allowed myself to daydream a little without being 'sensible' about it, there were vague but recurrent images of knives, and especially of blood. With a little more thought, following my dreams and daydreams for extra guidance, the connection became clear.

As a child in northern England in the 1950s, I was the older of two children. I was nearly three when my mother became pregnant with my sister. I have no recall of knowing this, or of what pregnancy was. These things were not talked about as they now are. Unknown to me until many years later, my mother developed a condition in mid-pregnancy which was dangerous and which required her to spend the final three months in a distant hospital. Again, by the very best parental thinking of the day, these were not things to worry a child about. One morning then, I awoke to find my mother gone, and a little set of toy cowboys and indians to play with in her place. Even now as I write about this I feel moved at the effort that Mum and Dad made trying to minimise the distress of this event. Hospitals were less humane places than now and child visitors were never allowed. My father had to keep working at his job, and could only travel to see my mother once a week himself, but each time he would bring a small toy from my mother. Thirty years later I can remember every detail of those toys. I imagine that Dad would have been quite distraught during those weeks, and I now know that children were acutely tuned in to such feelings. One bright day, though, we were reunited with Mum, pale and thin but quite alive, with a glowing new baby girl, and family life began again.

Back in the present, thirty years later, as I confronted my feelings, they came down to the unreasoned fear that Julie, being pregnant, would inexplicably disappear. Also that there would be blood, and that death was a possibility. The same thoughts that must have pre-occupied my father's mind, and been whispered above my head, thirty years before.

Since our job is helping people to locate and meet their unconscious needs, to 'heal the past in the present', the rest was simpler for us. *The first step is always to accept feelings as real, even if they do not make sense right away.* Everything in human beings makes sense eventually. Firstly we made an agreement not to be separated, physically, at any stage once the birth began (which itself lead to some major challenges as things worked out). Secondly, in the way that all parents should assure their children of *their* own safety, Julie affirmed that she would not die in childbirth. Strangely, I found that I could believe her. My fears subsided, and I could once again look forward to the birth.

Instances of the past mingling with the present, like the one given by Ian and Julie above, occur daily in our work with people undergoing changes in their lives. If we can recognise these intense reactions, and realise that they are just 'old stuff' resurfacing to be healed, then we can begin a major episode of self growth which will benefit us and our children. Whenever things go awry with families (and especially when good information and support do not seem to be helping as they should), then we look to the recycling mechanism to see if something is going on.

But I had a normal childhood

We live in a Freudian age, an age accustomed to thinking that if a person has problems, these probably stem from a traumatic or difficult childhood. Many people encounter great difficulties of living at some stage of their lives, yet have nothing extraordinary in their past on which to pin the blame! The group therapy sessions which were in vogue in the early 1970s always seemed to be full of people who had spent their childhood in concentration camps, been molested by grandfathers, or survived shipwrecks and so on. Those of us who felt equally isolated, anxious or uptight, but had no such excuse felt really defective!

If we had had a normal childhood, then we ought to be well adjusted. The problem in understanding one's own culture, of course, is to find a comparison. The more we have learned about childhood in other places and times, the clearer is the evidence that what we call normal in childrearing and parenthood, simply isn't. Examples of what could be called 'normal deprivation' abound. For instance infants growing up in the first half of the twentieth century did not get anywhere near enough touching, massage, or cuddling, and they certainly did not often get these basic forms of contact from relaxed and self-loving adults who could convey ease and security. A toddler was left alone for long periods, with little movement or stimulation. Schooling was heavily overstructured, with a hundred rules and restrictions, and the child was forced to sit still and concentrate on dull material. At home there were fears of failure, of not shaping up, of rejection in a performance-oriented value system. Later on in adolescence much basic information was withheld, leaving many youngsters riddled with personal doubts that had no basis in fact. These were the normal experiences. On top of this a child may have had other excesses or deficits—specific traumas like violence, incest, separations, deaths and griefs that were unexpressed, or constant hostility between parents in the days when divorce was a rarity. An emotionally adequate childhood in the people who have grown to be today's parents was a very rare thing. In spite of this, we grew up to be healthy, free, independent, well adjusted human beings. Well, almost!

If you grew up in these times (which will one day be looked on as a most aberrant phase of human family life) you did what human beings have always been good at — you survived. Eventually you grew up, formed relationships, and perhaps became a parent yourself. And the recycling process began. Right up to this present moment, the messages and memories just below the surface of everyday awareness, still continue to play out in our present-day life. And since the mind forever strives to be whole and in harmony, these wounds and puzzlements resurface again and again until we heal and understand. Let us share some examples.

Leonard was a tall, quiet man in one of our classes. He had a subtle sense of humour — a vibrant mind behind a shy exterior. He eventually did some work in the group, which was helpful to many others present, which we asked him to sum up for us later in writing:

> My father was gentle too, like I guess I am, but occasionally he would need to discipline us kids for some reason or other, which we no doubt deserved. When he became angry, he also got very shakey, and looked frightened — whether of us, or of his own anger, it was hard to tell. He could be verbally very harsh at these times too, and in fact a lot of the time made deprecatory remarks, though these would be said half as a joke. I grew up having no idea of how to be angry and not be frightened at the same time. The two were always mixed together. If I went into a shop to complain, I felt like apologising and making a donation!
>
> In the course of exploring this in the group, I recalled a time when my father had 'exploded' at home, and I, about seven at the time, had gone to bed in tears. My mother came to me and explained that Dad's own father had been exceptionally violent, in fact virtually demented, in the years following his return from the First World War. (Later he mellowed, so that I only knew my grandfather as a quite kindly, if gruff, old man.) My mother told me that my father had vowed, when he married her, that he would never hit her or their children, whatever happened.

I realised that this was something I could be grateful for. If my father had in fact gone too far in limiting his anger, and so become somewhat bitter, at least he was safe to be around. I had to now make my own progress — to learn not to be frightened of my own anger, and to assert myself in a balanced way. At last a lot of things made sense to me, and I knew what to do.

Leonard's was of course, another quite normal childhood! In our discussions of 'normal', we are of course speaking about the typical experience of Anglo-Saxon people, in western industrial countries. Our friends and trainees from Asian and Hispanic cultures report some of the same problems and some different ones. Some cultures (and some pockets within our own) never lost the traditional affection and naturalness with which children were treated in pre-industrial societies worldwide.

There are so many benefits of living in the safe and prosperous west, but we can also learn from the past and from elsewhere, adopting that which is of value. Birth is a clear and paradoxical example of just this. The most aware and assertive women of fifty years ago were demanding better hospital and health care for all women. Their granddaughters are now fighting a necessary battle to reduce medical interference and damage to the birth process. There is evidence that hospital birth has its own health hazards, some even feeling the need to stay at home to make their birth a safe one! We progress in such wide swings.

Key Stages in Your Life and Theirs

Most of the common hurdles of childrearing are hurdles precisely because they trigger recycling in us, the parents. Post-natal depression, the so called terrible twos, child-abuse, problems at school, mismanaged teenage sexuality, excluded fathers, career confusions — the whole litany begin to make more sense, and be more solvable, when seen in this light.

Let's examine some of these specific stages now. You may want to read straight on, or jump ahead to the stage that is currently making *your* life interesting.

Getting birth right

For a time in the western world, babies born in hospital were routinely taken away from their mothers to a 'nursery' at birth, so that 'mother could rest'. Other cultures would find this unthinkable, but somehow, in the overmedicalised decades from the 1940s onwards, it became the norm. Sometimes the babies would cry, others would mercifully sleep. Many would lie in a depressed state that was seen as being 'a good baby'. These days such practices are thankfully declining, as the commonsense of women reasserts itself over the whims and mystiques of medical fashion. The hospital practices of the twentieth century could not have been better designed to undermine the confidence, bonding and emotional integrity of the human family. The work of childbirth education movement, women such as Penelope Leach and Sheila Kitzinger, and doctors like Frederic Leboyer, Michel Odent and others, has met with acclaim among parents largely because it confirms a deep intuitive sense about how birth should be. Such obvious changes as freedom to give birth in a comfortable posture, the presence of fathers and support people, the avoidance of unnecessary procedures (such as routine cutting, chemical inductions or unwarranted Caesarians), and of course the mother and child remaining together after the birth, are finally being affirmed as a right.

Bonding to both parents just after birth is very easy, especially if accompanied by skin-to-skin contact, natural smells, and the chance for the infant to immediately suckle. The first thirty minutes of life can create in the newborn child an internal sense of safety and a trust that will be a foundation for every aspect of family life from there on. We know from our work with families that interrupted bonding can be gradually rebuilt later, but why rupture the bonding process in the first place?

The disruptive nature of hospital birth practices over approximately the last three generations has lead to a recycling issue for many women entering new parenthood. Mothers who were born under the old regime are now grown to adulthood and are having babies of their own. One theory of post-natal depression is that it is caused by recycling of the mother's own birth separation. In her own early infancy, the mother may have experienced the first hours of life as full of despair and abandonment — pushed from the pulsating, secure holding of the womb to suddenly be alone and still, perhaps the only sound now being the disturbed cries of other inmates of the sterile, glaringly-lit nursery. None of this, of course, is consciously remembered by the adult mother. But as she now gives birth herself, the smells, sensations and primitive memories recall her own birth scene, and as her baby is taken from her body, a sense of deep emptiness may sweep over her.

The effect of recycling one's own birth may range from simple tearfulness, through to depression and, for some, to a full blown loss of contact with reality. The syndrome known as post-natal depression is common and widespread in western countries, yet in many other cultures it is virtually unknown. Dozens of mothers we have spoken with have supported this theory from their own experiences. It is an area which needs much further study.

Whatever the cause of PND is held to be, we believe it is best treated by validating the feelings and needs of the new mother, and responding to these in a human way. The new mother needs to be mothered herself, massaged, comforted, fed, cared for by people she loves, not left alone (or even in the care of strangers) unless she expressly wishes. She must have her baby close at all times. This is especially important for a Caesarian birth. If a new mother decides she is not yet able to manage this, she must know that someone she knows and trusts is with the baby caring for it, able to bring it to her at any time.

Common treatment for PND in the past has been a combination of antidepressants and exhortations, ranging from patronising to the downright cruel 'pull yourself together'. We are convinced that 'mothering the mother', in a very physical sense, is the most effective way to heal her separation trauma, so that she can 'grow up' again rapidly herself, and then be an emotionally available parent to her child. If you have done what you can in preparation, so as to be in charge of your birth situation, and are nonetheless thrown into an 'upset' regressive state after giving birth, accept this as a healing of your own deep hurts. Allow yourself to ask those around you for the caring you may need in the weeks that follow.

Like many so-called 'disorders' of modern life, PND may be simply an extreme of what we all feel at times — simply the reflection of how lonely and unsupported parenting has become in our culture. Because of the deep ruptures in our nurturing experience, sometimes recycled across many generations, some individuals are more prone to apparent collapse under the practical and hormonal stress of new parenthood. As we learn to value and support both fatherhood and motherhood, and treat these as privileged and worthy roles, the mantle of new parenthood will rest more lightly on all of our shoulders. Soon there will be a new sense of power and rightness about being a mother.

Preventing post-natal depression

Prevention of PND, and the formation of a strong mother/child bond, hinges on reinforcing the mother-to-be as an *adult*, and not a dependent child. We've often heard gynaecologists refer to their patients as 'all my girls'. This is usually a giveaway to a rather patronising attitude. Medical practitioners in this field are often superb technicians, as well as kind and dedicated to the safe delivery of babies, but their training has rarely equipped them to work in partnership with mothers and fathers as equals.

Similarly nurses who feel that they know better than young parents how to care for their newborns, and intervene from this position, can sabotage the confidence of the new parent. In some hospitals nurses slip babies a formula feed while in the nursery, specifically against the orders of the parent, and to the direct detriment of the establishment of a breastfeeding routine. This is not just a moral invasion, but more importantly for hospitals, an illegal action, and will hopefully decline. Even the giving of unsolicited advice can be damaging to parental confidence. Though well intentioned, and in the usual sense 'correct', advice will have a negative effect if it erodes the person's own exploratory steps into parenthood. More and more, though, we are delighted to watch hospital and child health staff gracefully supporting the learning process of young parents, resisting the urge to interfere, only offering help and advice when there is an expressed need, so that confidence can grow unimpaired.

By their very nature, hospitals tend to impose passivity and loss of control. It's embedded in the language: we are 'admitted' and are 'delivered of' a baby by a team of technicians. We are 'allowed to take baby home' (in whatever number of days is the 'hospital policy'). Meanwhile a Ugandan mother-to-be pauses in her work in the fields and with quiet excitement calls the nearby women around her — women who have known her all her life. She squats in the shade of a tree, and squeezes out a bright-eyed child. In a day or two the child is strapped to her back, as she continues to work. (Uganda is just a random example. However, studies of pre-school children in that country showed dramatic motor-skills and perceptial advancement over their western counterparts.

The stories we hear of easy natural childbirth in other cultures can't all be the wishful thinking of hippy anthropologists. Labour is just the right word for the process of birth — sometimes easy, sometimes very hard work, for some a comfortable process, for others painful. Since we are creating a new life, it somehow seems appropriate that demands should be made of us in the process.

What parents object to increasingly is not the effort of birth, but the indignity and loss of control that go with this in a medical setting. It seems eminently desirable to be adult about giving birth, and to approach it with self-assurance. To be allowed to be *in charge* of one's environment and what happens in it. Why can't we have the security of medical resources *and* control over the manner in which we give birth — surely one of the most important acts of our whole lives? We are delighted these days to find at almost every gathering of parents we attend, two new phenomena. We hear fathers everywhere these days enthusing about the experience of the birth, a life-event from which twenty years ago they would have been forcibly excluded, if they had even thought or wished to attend. And where once older women seemed to take almost malicious pleasure in passing on negative tales about birth, the stories are now of enjoyment, hard work, physical achievement and self-pride.

Birth is one of the three or four really big things you can do in a human lifetime, and if the year before and the year after are spent doing nothing else but supporting the changes, then it is time well spent.

Men becoming fathers

On the cover of John Cleese's superb book *Families and How to Survive Them* is a cartoon of a father watching his wife with a new baby at the breast — a peaceful domestic scene. But the father's expression is rather depressed, and in his mouth is a dummy! Herein lies a tale.

Fathers who were firstborns, or came from big families, or families where babies were adored and toddlers disliked, often receive a recycled shock when their wives have a baby. The mother–baby bond always impinges on a husband–wife bond to some degree, but many men feel as if 'that's it', their marriage is over! An understanding of the recycled feelings surfacing here is helpful in order for fathers to relax again.

Let us backtrack a little to illustrate where fathering problems often arise. A recent TV current affairs program featured a story about a boy with 'tantrum problems'. The particular show is not known for its depth of coverage, so it mainly concentrated on the dramatic footage — tantrums in supermarkets, assaults on parents with broomsticks, and so on. However, casually mentioned over a brief shot was the small but important detail that a new baby girl had recently been born in the family. Watching the baby breastfeed, the little boy was not at all angry or tantrumming, but sat rocking and distressed, repeatedly crying that he wanted a bottle. His mother's words were revealing. 'You're a big boy now' she rebuked. She was doing the best she knew, reflecting the common belief system 'grow up kid, you're not the baby any more'. However, this kind of sudden change in a child's family status can clearly lead not only to behaviour problems at the time, but to recycled problems when the child grows to be a father himself. The 'experts' interviewed on the show waxed on about behaviour modification and seemed to gravely miss the point. Toddlers often feel little and vulnerable with a new arrival. With a little allowance for this and some sharing of affection, they will grow up to actually *like* babies, and not see them as competition. Sometimes 'experts' cause us to despair!

If a new father has strong childhood memories (conscious or unconscious) of being supplanted by another new arrival, and of losing primacy because his parents switched their affections too sharply, then that father will have some definite 'carry-over' emotional needs which should be met. He will need to be assured verbally and physically, just as the woman needs to be assured, that he is primary in his partner's affections, and will remain so in thought, if not in allocation of time (for a while). Kids' needs are big at the beginning, and diminish over time, while partnerships are a long-term investment. This reassurance can be reciprocal, and both partners will need to maintain lovingness rituals at a time when sleep is broken, recreation reduced, and sexual relations are variable to say the least! It sounds terrible! Couples find that they can make their lives and loving more time effective in all sorts of ways and that no-one needs to miss out as the new family unit settles into shape.

Mothering and fathering are distinct and different. All human beings need both. Fathers who were not fathered themselves may not even know how to play with children and enjoy their company. Experiment a little if you're in this category. The key to playing with children is to find out what you can *both* enjoy. The model train industry thrives on this dynamic! Find the childhood pleasure of play alongside your kids, recycling a new childhood for yourself at the same time.

> I'm a little older than the average father, and found it hard to be with my kids in an enjoyable way. I tried for a while to get interested in finger-painting and Lego, but I'm not that kind of guy. I'd end up irritable with the kids and walk off! Then I decided to come at it from the other angle. I like fishing, and gardening and computers. I decided to work at sharing these interests. When we went fishing, I'd snag the line, and then pretend that we had a big one on the hook, and me and the kids pulled and played and wound until the line snapped. They were so excited! The next hurdle was not to have to achieve anything. I had to relax my old criteria of being productive. We would 'waste' time in that nothing would get done, but we'd have fun. If I wanted to actually catch fish, or plant garden beds, then I'd do it another time by myself! When my work colleagues talk about not understanding their kids, not being able to get close to them, I think — well, right now me and the kids know how to have a good time together. They're just toddlers now, but some of that must continue as they get older. I hope so.

Don't be with your children from a sense of guilt or sacrifice, unless this is the only way you can get started! Look for how you can enjoy them. Especially for a burnt-out career-driven father, kids may literally give you a new lease of life, reviving your physical health as well as reordering your priorities for living.

We hear more and more men these days state that fathering is one of the most enjoyable, most satisfying things they ever did! This is an enormous change of viewpoint in the space of perhaps two generations, and will profoundly improve the emotional health of generations to come.

The challenge of twoness

We're not endeared to labels like 'terrible twos', but twoness, let's face it, is different. It isn't really an age but a state of mind, an unfolding of *will* in the personality of the growing child. It can appear for the first time at any age from one to thirteen. What it means is that the child is developing character! Anyone can love a baby that sits around and grins and goos. But to become a 'person' requires a little conflict and some struggling with limitations.

Any healthy child will sooner or later try you out in a big way, and you will need to learn how to 'hang loose' and 'stand up for yourself', all at the same time. If your discipline tends to be heavy-handed and mean, your child may get scared and quit, then later get hyped up and angry back at you. If your style is often to back down to their demands, paradoxically this scares them too, and they will escalate until you *have to* say no. Once again, consciously, this is all common sense, but where life gets interesting is if your own two-year-old experiences get in the way. If *your* parents handled your twoness by being vindictive, angry or mean, then you will associate fear with any conflict situation. If you-at-two walked all over mum and dad, that wouldn't have taught you much either: you will have tape recordings only of how to back down, and no recordings of how to be 'relaxed but *firm*'.

Overcoming niceness

Both kinds of imbalance in parenting originate in fear feelings. One way some people have of handling fear is to develop a manner usually called 'niceness'! 'Nice' people handle the discomfort of conflict by backing away from it. When dealing with children a skill at diverting from conflict is handy, but some straight out saying of *no* is essential as preparation for the real world. If niceness has been your style, it probably pervades your life. You're probably nice to literally everyone: you feel sorry for used car salesmen and think well of politicians. If someone burgles your video, you run after them with the remote controller! Niceness can work for a while in adult life, but with children it goes badly wrong. The conflict doesn't go away. Parenting is, perhaps for the first time in your life, something you can't back out of! You smile pleasantly, grit your teeth, try harder, talk sweetly, and then *explode*! Moments later you're filled with shame and remorse, and the cycle recommences. Aaargh!

Another problem with niceness is that it gives no security. Kids actually seem to create conflict in order to get an intense reaction from you, to test if you are real. Listen to this perceptive young father speaking.

> When our son Zeb was three, my wife Allie went away to India for four weeks, and I took care of him. It was a chance to prove my fathering skills! We wondered if he'd miss his mum, but things went quite well. One day he didn't eat his dinner, but asked for a honey sandwich. I refused. He needed to eat something better than that. He whinged and whined and clambered about and messed up the food on his plate. I chickened out and gave him a honey sandwich. So what did he do then? He changed his mind! He wanted a peanut butter sandwich, and threw the honey sandwich on the floor! That was enough for me. I yelled at him, and put him in the corner. When he was ready, he came out, said sorry and started to eat his meat and vegetables. I told him he was a great kid, and he started to cry. 'I want Mummy to be back now!'. I said 'It's sad to miss her isn't it? It hurts sometime?' and he said yes. After tea he devised a game where he was with Mummy, in India (under a rug) and told me I'd have to cry because he is on holiday. Then he came back, and cuddled me. It was all very interesting.

It's an old cliché that kids need rules to feel secure. Perhaps they also need fights with mum and dad to help them with the struggles they are having on the inside—necessary struggles since the world is not always gentle or fair. A child can use the robust contacts and disagreements that adults offer to strengthen and integrate his or her own self in the face of occasional hardship. Parents who are tough and tender at the same time produce courageous yet sensitive children in turn.

Nastiness doesn't pay

While some parents in the past have been over-mushy with discipline, others find themselves becoming, in a word, 'nasty'. No-one chooses this, but if you feel threatened at times by children's disobedience, and then cover your fear by getting angry instead of assertive, emotional instead of good humoured, then nastiness is the result. We all know the signs: when your smack has an edge to it, and your grabs are just a little too hard for the purpose.

> I got pulled up short. As she was crying after I'd smacked her, she said through her sobs 'Mummy that was a mean smack to me!'.

Adults who get nasty are experiencing the child as competition, and are interpreting their non co-operation as a personal attack. They seek to counter-attack so as to destroy the threat, but it's such an unfair contest. From a child's perspective, this makes for a world which is cruel and scary, and you know how bad that feels to a child, because you've been there too. Don't pass it on.

The way out of the apparent double bind of nasty or nice is to do 'none of the above'. It is a mistake to say 'I'll never be like my parents were to me' and go to the other extreme, and equally misguided to unthinkingly run out the old methods you were given, and take historic revenge.

Instead, begin to become conscious of yourself. Notice your feelings, before they are strong and dominant. How can you get more comfortable, right now? Perhaps some clear self talk is all it needs: 'I don't need to feel afraid of children. They're normal, they sometimes need some firmness, that's all!'. In addition to this, you can begin to surface your unconscious feelings and accept and 'clear' these constantly, as they arise, while at the same time not letting them come between the real here-and-nowness of *you* and *your child*.

> When Sara misbehaves, I get a feeling in my stomach and head that is so uncomfortable. It's as if my own mother is watching me, over

my shoulder, and saying 'You're doing it wrong. You'll ruin that child', and that makes me feel worse — angry and inadequate at the same time.'

Another parent comments:

My father wouldn't say much when we played up as kids — just grab the nearest one and belt into him. You never knew when he would do it, or for what reason — just for making a noise, or laughing too loudly in the bedroom. When *my* kids act up, all I know is I don't want to be like Dad. I get frightened that I will lash out, and my discipline seems very uneven to me.

As parents identify where their old feelings come from, and talk about these, they are well on the way to separating the past from the present.

Child abuse is the meeting of a defiant, frightened real life child, and an adult who is taken over by the frightened child inside him or her. It's a fight between two two-year-olds, of whom one is dangerously bigger.

Therapists, especially those experienced in what is called the redecision method, can greatly speed this process of healing your child inside. You don't have to be in therapy to heal yourself though. Think about, and spend time reflecting on, your own twoness memories, however faint they are. Notice your body reactions when your child defies you, and do what you can to make yourself comfortable. When you are hyped up, do something vigorous. Physical activity will work to discharge the adrenaline build-up left after tackling an unreasonable child. Our house is often cleaned, and the lawns mercilessly cut, on the strength of such encounters!

One thing always needs to be stated clearly. It is wrong to hit children in anger. You know this because even though there is a release in hitting, there is also guilt and the child feels hurt and untrusting. It becomes harder to gain trust and co-operation next time without increased threat. Hitting children is the original vicious circle. So what are better ways?

Firmness is easy (when you know how)

The following are brief clues to being firm with children.

1   The first step is to minimise conflict potential. Avoid boredom for both you and the child. Variety in your day, having other kids to play (though don't expect sharing or real co-operative play until three or four years of age), and just plenty of chances to expend energy, all help.

2   The second step is how you use words. When you say no you must mean it. End of argument. You must say exactly what you want, when you want it, and not take no for an answer. Physically remove your child from the problem when necessary, until they get the message.

3   The third step is 'the corner'. What children are doing from eighteen months to three years (and beyond), is learning to *think* their way through life's situations. Many 'experts' (especially those not personally involved with children) recommend behaviour modification techniques — 'star charts', and 'time out' and so on. These methods, derived from rat psychology, do not address the central purpose in children's development at this stage, which is to learn to think. Behaviour modification is useful in its place, but without communication all you get is well trained rats! What is needed is a way to make children uncomfortable when they transgress, but also a way to help them to learn rapidly and intelligently why they should change, and how.

The corner technique is a way to help children listen and think, and is enormously useful, not to humiliate or punish, but to teach a child how to figure problems out. They must stand in the corner, where you can place them facing towards the wall. They do this *only* until they can say (a) what they were doing wrong and (b) that they are sorry. If they don't know, tell them, and ask them to tell you back. If they say sorry but aren't, then let them know this, and come back in a minute.

After they have mastered the above steps fairly well, and as they get a little older, ask them to say something else they could do next time to avoid a repeat of the problem. If they are stuck, give them a suggestion. 'Next time you want some attention, you don't hit me, you say 'Excuse me Mummy I want you. Now, what will you do next time?'

Be clear with children in the corner that they do not have to feel bad, or cry, but just think and apologise when they are ready to. They can call you as soon as they are ready to 'deal'. They can't come out of the corner, until they call you and things are fixed up. We emphasise again that this is not punishment, it is teaching, and there is no need for you to be angry or for them to feel 'not okay'.

We don't use the corner in front of other kids or adults much, because it can be embarrassing for the child, but will take the child into another room if need be. We use the word 'deal' – 'you need to *deal* with what you just did', to sum up the process in the child's mind. Soon they will 'deal' with things like apologies, or agreed behaviour in different circumstances, without the need for the corner, just a verbal reminder. Natural consequences are a part of dealing too – helping clean up a mess they have made, saying sorry to a child they hurt in overexuberant play and so on. There is no 'naughtiness' in children of this age, unless they have been handled in vindictive ways. There is a vast amount of inappropriate action though, as this is the time when the child first learns self-control, and can only do so by trial and error. Be prepared to stay good humoured through a lot of repetition!

4   The fourth step is 'time out' – taking children to their rooms and leaving them there for a short time. On occasions when the corner is not being used well by the child, usually if the child is just too hyped up, then time out (five minutes maximum) is the final back-up. Usually as with the corner, they can tell you when they are ready to come out, though when you are angry and need time it can be when you are ready. Going to their room (or often being carried protesting) is also useful if children won't stand in the corner but treat it as a game. When they are ready to come out they call you, go to the corner, deal with the problem, and then are free again!

We only use time out as a back-up, or when *we* need a break. When children are struggling to solve problems, then isolation is the last thing they need.

Whatever your form of discpline, it should end with the child thinking through the problem, and reconciliation.

Other causes of inappropriate action

Finally, there are physical causes to watch for too. During toddlerhood our son would become significantly more energised (that's the nicest word we can find for it!) if he had just consumed chocolate or refined sugar, or certain artificially coloured foodstuffs. Many parents have noted similar (but varying) triggers to their children becoming suddenly harder to manage. Watch out for what your child reacts to, and without getting obsessive about it, make the changes to diet that help you and them stay peaceful.

Be loving and tolerant towards yourself, as well as your child, and this phase will develop in you a whole new equilibrium. Once you can handle two-year-olds, you can handle anyone!

Finally, we need to remember that twoness is not all about conflict. Children at this age are more exploratory, self-sufficient, and physically easier to care for. Make sure that you give yourself more freedom and enjoyment now that they are out of the babyhood phase, so that you and your child do more independent and outgoing kinds of activities, both separately and together. There's a big world just waiting for both of you.

This is the world, I'll show you how it works

After you've met the first testing of the two-year-old phase (and proved you can take it!) you and your child can now shift the focus outwards. Your role changes to a new one which will carry right through to the teenage years, that of *the parent as teacher about life*. Just as you are feeding a little body to make it big, you are feeding a little mind with what it needs to be fully adult. The constant criteria will be 'How would this behaviour work in the big world!' and 'What does my child need to understand about this in order to fully honour him or herself, and the world of other people?'.

Through a myriad of different issues and concerns, right through the primary school years, the guiding principle remains clear: 'What behaviour and understanding does this child need to learn, so as to be happy and belong in the adult world?'. Many parents in the past directed and disciplined their children only from a 'defensive' position, reacting only if the child annoyed or intruded on them.

J. WRIGHT

Parenting can be much more active, and much more positive than this. Why wait till you're annoyed?

Take one common example—whingeing. Whingeing is carefully designed by your child to be so irritating that you give in to it. Do you know an adult that whinges? Do you like his or her company? This behaviour has got to go! Tell your children how they sound, and that they need to use a normal voice if they want a response.

After the two-year-old struggle phase, the 'trusting threes' come like an oasis of calm (sometimes!). Remember that even though children become delightfully sociable and imitative, they are not just little people—they are still young, needing affection and playfulness just as much. New intense feelings also arise about what is fair and who is boss. Three- and four-year-olds provoke fights in order to release fears and angers. Teach them to use words to express feelings, in fact insist that they do. Let them know that they can be angry, and scared, and sad, and say so.

Fantasy becomes a major way of learning. Four-year-olds are full of 'What ifs . . .?'. Teach them that fantasy and reality are distinct. They can make things up, and so why not make things up that feel good, or exciting. Play monster games with them, and take turns to be the monster. This way children concretely take charge of their fearful projections.

Planning and commitments matter a lot in adult life. Teach pre-school children to have jobs around the house which they must remember. They must learn to take turns.

Five-to-seven-year-olds are learning about three-way relationships, and will play you off against your partner. Be amicable but unconned by this. 'Nice try!' you say, 'but you heard what I said the first time'. Parents may have to sort out differences in approach here so as to stay on top!

Seven-to-ten-year-olds must internalise a great number of rules, since by now they have moved well beyond our supervision. They already love to hassle and argue. Their favourite word may be 'but'. Parents have to remain unthreatened by this. It isn't insurrection (well, not completely!), just an overwhelming urge in the child to have things sorted out. They will provoke us to apply and enforce the rule, not so as to get away with breaking it, but so that we will give a firm and secure response. In this way children learn how to be firm and secure in themselves. The issues are little things like 'being on time' and 'keeping your side of the bargain'.

All of the above require us adults to have clear ideas of how to manage life, often clearer than we actually have formulated for ourselves! We find that lots of time is now taken up with talking with other parents about how they do things. Recycling constantly keeps us learning as we go along. It's lucky that kids go to school — it gives us time to regroup!

One difficulty is that we have to live up to our teaching. If you have made a fuss about being on time, and you are late to pick up your eight-year-old from school, how do you deal with it? A sneaky excuse? An aggressive brush off? Watch out now, you're on Child Camera! 'I'm sorry, Gerry. I tried to get some shopping on the way and it took longer than I thought. Next time I'll leave the shopping until I've got you, okay?'

'Oh, okay!'

Everyone makes mistakes. Adults own them, and fix them.

By about age ten, things have often become relatively quiet and manageable. Meteorologically this is called the centre of the cyclone. Enjoy it, a good foundation has been laid, which will be added to and built on in the next few years. When the teens arrive, there is an easy formula to apply: subtract twelve from your child's age! This will give a good approximate guide to their developmental stage, which they are now recycling for the first time. Adolescence, while being a whole new phase in itself, offers a *second chance* to rework all the thinking, feeling and behaviour lessons of the first twelve years. We hope you'll see this as a cheering thought! (This is a whole book in itself, and we're working on it.)

Achievements and ambitions (whose life is it anyway?)

There's a lot of money to be made by the first person to market piano lessons, not for kids, but for their culturally ambitious parents! A vast industry exists teaching children what parents 'wished they could have had the chance to learn', and we think it would solve a lot of heartache if parents could fulfil their *own* dreams, and not impose them on the next generation. Along with parental piano practice could go special parents' football teams, and big-little athletics meetings where overweight, loud-mouthed folks could be put into shorts and T-shirts and herded into gruelling activity. Children could then be left to pursue the non-competitive, non-sexist, free-flowing activity that they naturally create for themselves, given half a chance.

The advertising industry, the fashion industry, even toy manufacturers, and a number of self-interested sporting bodies, are all doing their best to completely eradicate childhood! You may need to protect your child's space and time to just be a child.

The school years are all about discovering your own sense of direction. This should develop gradually in the form of choices of activities and competencies which each young person will want to follow, that will be uniquely his or her own. Even after the most regimented or dominated childhood, all human beings at some time in their lives make the break for self-regulation, for literally taking charge of their own lives. The surge of selfhood first appears at two to three years of age (with issues like eating and dressing), it simmers along through school and play activities, recycles more powerfully again at thirteen to fifteen, and will re-emerge again and again until properly completed.

In previous generations, the urge for freedom often seemed close to being crushed by economic necessity and a culture of exceptional conformity, but somehow the urge for individuality reasserts itself over and over again. The so-called mid-life crisis is not a natural or necessary stage as claimed by some writers: it is primarily experienced only by people who've spent half a lifetime doing 'what was expected'. Remember that much societal and family pressure to conform is unspoken, and is therefore for the most part an unconscious experience. The young person may honestly feel and exclaim 'Well, I do *want* to be a doctor' (but the sun is shining outside), and the parents counter-exclaim 'We *only* want what's best for you' (now how about you get back and do some studying). We've often heard kids and adults simply lose track of their own wishes and exclaim in despair 'What *do* I want?'.

Many school teachers and school counsellors report that the over-directed youngster, the teenager (or younger child) who is heavily or subtly being programmed to someone else's idea of a good life, usually at some stage has a study-crisis, or even a health-crisis which prevents them from carrying out their parents' ambitions for them. Thus they can be free to pursue their own career. Parents need to self-search a little to find out if this is happening to their child, and if such crises occur, to use them to free up and give more leeway to youngsters. The alternative is more serious crises in an attempt (usually unconscious) to get free. We think that it's much better to have this 'start-life' crisis while you're in mid-stream educationally with choices and decisions easier to reverse, than halfway through your life (though better late than never).

We heard one child say 'They keep telling me education is to prepare me for living. But I *am* living.' *The purpose of education is to find out what you really love to do.* We are learning slowly, as a culture, to foster children's innate sense of what they need and where their hearts lie, and to have trust in the choices they make.

Teenage sexuality (aargh!)

There is something especially beautiful about teenagers. You get to see glimpses of the kind of adult that they are on the way to being, but at the same time there is a fresh, intense clarity about them which makes you feel good about life. Idealistic, intense, emotional, physical, and of course sexy! And this latter quality is sometimes one which parents find hard to handle. There are potent unconscious recyclings going on here too! Our favourite story about this is from a friend of ours, who as a teenage girl received very little information about puberty and sex, and so had the usual confused and scary time. She vowed she would never withhold information from her own children about sex and biology. She was a little surprised how soon the chance came though, when her three-year-old asked her one day 'Where va children come fwom?'.

Our friend immediately swung into Operation Full and Honest Disclosure. With copies of *Everywoman*, *A Child is Born*, *The Joy of Sex*, and so on, she sat on the floor and gave a thorough and detailed explanation. Into the second half hour, she noticed the toddler glazing over a little, but continued undeterred. History was being put to rights! Finally she asked the littlie if she now had a satisfactory answer to her question. The child said no! It turned out mum had answered the wrong question. Since they lived near a school, each afternoon a stream of kids came past their front gate, and the little girl just wanted to know 'Where va children come fwom?'!

Our fears for teenagers stay fears if they are never voiced out loud. Parents and children wander needlessly in a sea of unknowns. Talking can sometimes dispel needless fears (leaving you to concentrate on the real ones!). Few topics are as fear-evoking for parents as sex. If we fear teenage pregnancy in particular, we can easily end up radiating mistrust like a lighthouse, and so drive kids' natural openness underground. You need to talk about such things. The bravest, most honest way to connect with your teenage son or daughter is to talk about your own adolescent experiences, including the failures and mistakes, and what you learned from them. Do so casually, as they come up in conversation, rather than having a sudden, serious sit-down-and-talk.

Later you may want to let them know about specific concerns or experiences that were hard for you. This shouldn't take the form of a sermon. It's a sharing, and will invite their honesty. If you are fearful for them, say so. This is not equal to mistrust (though they may try that one on you!). If you feel too emotional to discuss an issue with your teenager, talk to a friend first until your emotions settle down and your head clears. Tom Gordon, founder of the parent effectiveness movement, points out that true anger (the wish to push away and hurt) is rarely a primary feeling between a parent and child, whereas anger used to cover fear is often present, and very destructive. If you are frightened by what is happening to your child, say so, but allow that your fears may be groundless, or not shared by your kids. Realise, and spell out, the positive messages that you love them and want them to care for themselves effectively. Leave the specifics to them. *Open talking with youngsters leads to clearer thinking, which leads to more considered action, which is what counts.* Adolescence is about making your own decisions, so don't be dogmatic. Let go!

Remember you will be recyling your own teens as you parent your teenagers. The challenge, as always, is to be aware of where you are coming from. Teenagers can be happy, beautiful to the eye, mobile, free, sociable and, if not as sexually active as we imagine, then certainly glowing as if they are. These things have a marked effect on middle-aged parents. Very likely you may feel jealous, and if you acknowledge this to yourself, then there's no problem. Unacknowledged though, jealousy curdles into bitter restrictiveness or immature competition. Go out and do some of the things *you* always wanted to (well, some of them) and at least be an example of some joy in living. At the same time be self-caring and thoughtful in areas like your own alcohol use, and your own sexual responsibility, so that there is role-modelling available. The aim is that your watchful teenager is not embarrassed by you but just slightly, grudgingly, impressed by your style.

Remember that with teenagers as with partners 'What you notice is what you get'. A couple attending a 'Living with Teenagers' workshop told us: 'Our kids are totally out of control!'.

'How do you mean?' we asked.

'We set a curfew of one a.m., they come home at two. If we make it two they come in at three.'

We asked 'How come they are so reliable?'.

'Huh?'

'They're very regular! An hour late every time! Why do they come home at all? Why not next morning? Why haven't they sold your video for drugs? How many abortions have they had?'

'They're not *that* bad!'

Ultimately there is only one way to help your children be happy in love and life, and that is to pursue these same goals yourself, with courage, care and optimism. If *you* don't make adulthood look like a drag, your kids will *want* to grow up. If you are honest about its difficulties, they will not want to rush into it headlong.

There is no other way to be a good parent of teenagers than to find day-to-day happiness yourself, and pass this on as you go.

Excuse Me While I Grow Myself Up

A woman once took her young son to see Mahatma Ghandi. She asked if he would tell her son not to eat sweets, as he was getting fat. Ghandi told her to go away and come back in a week. She did this, and then he told the boy 'don't eat sweets'. The boy looked suitably impressed (after all, this was the man who took India off the British!). The woman did not leave, though, as she stood mumbling, and Ghandhi-ji asked 'What is it now?'.

She said 'I don't want to sound ungrateful, but why the week?'.

'Oh', replied Ghandi, 'I never like to tell other people to do what I can't do myself. It took me all week to get off the sweets!'

The half-dozen transitions we've mentioned in this chapter are only some of the many typical challenges that families pass through. The fact that childhood changes also require growth in the parents, once acknowledged, makes things much more comprehensible. Through all of this discussion, it is important to remember that recycling is not a mystical event. It is purely physical, triggered by certain stimuli — the sights, sounds, words, and smells associated with the age your children are passing through. One way to use this awareness is to simply ask yourself on 'bad' days or difficult times 'How old am I feeling right now?' and then organise some of what you need (and needed at that age) in order to feel good. If you feel like a baby, baby yourself. If you feel restricted, organise some space for freedom. Use your kids' needs and reactions as a clue: little children fire off one set of responses, teenagers another. You will find that parenthood becomes literally a return trip through your own childhood, in slow episodes, teaching and healing you all the way.

Conscious parenting

Through the process of recycling, you will grow yourself up — hopefully just ahead of your children. Newborns will help you to learn to feel safe in the world, so that you can pass this on to them. The care of a totally vulnerable little child will show you the preciousness of life. Toddlers will teach you about independence and dealing with limits. Two-year-olds will teach you how to be assertive. School age children will light you up to the creative and exploratory possibilities of the world. Teenagers will rekindle your sociability, your wish to be free, and perhaps even your sexuality.

Grown children leaving home will remind you of endings and mortality (and also set you free for another half a lifetime!)

Even if you do nothing overtly or deliberately, the awareness of this process will change what is happening for you, and your children, for the better. You *will* do a better job than your parents did for you, because you will build on the start you were given. There will be surprises as old memories and the feelings anchored to them fire off in your brain cells and add richness to the things that happen in the here-and-now. Much recycling is positive. If adults delighted in you as a young person, it is nostalgic delight to pass on the same permissions and praise to your own and other youngsters.

The secret of parenthood, and partnering, is to be increasingly and intensely self-aware, to be attuned to your own growing edge, so that your actions, rather than being driven and reactive, are conscious and deliberately chosen. If anything like us, you will react automatically, off the cuff, in ways you don't much like, many times a day. That's okay! The kids and situations will just keep on recurring till you get it right. (Isn't that helpful of them!)

Give up on perfection. Be happy to be a learner. If the Buddhists are right, when you are perfect you die! Where's the fun in that? Simply do the best you can at the time. The human race is a relay race in which you do your sprint and then pass on the baton. Your parents did their best, you'll do your part as consciously as you can, your kids will do theirs, and our whole two-legged, furry-headed species will make its way onwards!

CHAPTER 5

The Sex-Romance Alliance

We: *Well, it's been a couple of months since we saw you. You're both looking great!*

He: *Things **are** good now. We've got some spare money at last, we've sold the house, the kids are okay . . . and we're even talking to each other again.*

She: *Yes, we're doing **everything** again!*

We: *You mean you'd stopped having sex?*

He: *Oh no, it never quite got **that** bad!*

Understand Love and You Understand Life

As advanced as our generation has become in understanding human relations, we have copped out badly when it comes to explaining love. We have left ourselves, and our children, to choose between something vague and mysterious that happens to you, love that you catch (like a disease), or else love as banal, the feeling that you have towards cheesecake or Turkish delight. No wonder that people end up not believing in the one, and being bored with the other.

In this chapter we hope to go a step better than this. We want to confirm the existence of love, and explore its dynamics in realistic terms. We're convinced that loving (oneself, the world and other people) is the most logical and appropriate way to respond to life.

After developing this point, in a brief digression to the world of philosophy, we will then move on to how love is brought into one's personal life, so that romantic love — which we call the sex-romance alliance — can enhance not just rare moments by accident, but your whole life, by design.

How to be realistic

There is a way of looking at the world, much in fashion these days, that sees everything through jaded eyes. Cynicism is the norm, and any deviation from this is therefore regarded with suspicion. Being cynical tends, though, to make much of life seem drab, disappointing, grey and ugly. Pleasure comes only by escaping the world briefly, literally through 'diversions'. People who share this perception call themselves realistic, rational, sensible, worldly. They pride themselves on having reality pretty much pinned down (as they reach for another drink to soften the blow).

There are other ways of perceiving reality. While popular science seems to reduce the world to the level of the banal, some scientists — Albert Einstein, Gregory Bateson, David Suzuki, James Lovelock and Rupert Sheldrake, for instance — have written works that sound more like poetry. There are papers in respected journals on the universe behaving more like a thought than a machine, that all time is happening at once, that all life on the earth acts as one organism, that the universe has life programmed into it, and so on. Scientists do not see the world as ordinary at all.

There are two competing ways of thinking about life, for the surprising reason that our brain has two distinct hemispheres. The two co-operate by shuttling back and forth rapidly, but are nonetheless distinct, and can even be separated surgically (though we don't recommend this!) Logical thought mostly takes place in the left hemisphere of our brain. Feelings and intuitions, creativity and inventiveness live in the right. Our 'mind' shifts from one side to the other as we think, feel, intuit and deduct our way through a problem.

This division of our brains is the reason, for instance, why it is very hard to keep worrying (which uses the left brain) while listening to beautiful music (which uses the right). It is emerging from brain research that linear left-brained thought, is fine for day-to-day stuff like catching the bus, counting change, fixing a car. Using this capacity, our culture has been able to put men on the moon (now gone home), and build and target 60,000 nuclear missiles (still there). Neglecting the other half of the brain, we have tended not to address the really big questions like 'Why?' When it comes to the important things such as the nature of life, light, atomic physics, time, ecology, and getting along with the opposite sex, logic fails almost every time.

People have as blind a faith in science as they once had in religion. As a child in school the impression you were no doubt given was that science had reality pretty well sewn up. There were a few little details (and the odd gaping hole) still to be explored, but basically they (the experts) knew what was going on in this life of ours. The teachers, and more importantly, the TV shows, used words like 'modern', 'advanced', 'scientific progress', 'research proves . . .', and like good children, we believed them. This, of course, was exactly the sort of thing that was taught to children in 2000 B.C. (the world is made of five elements), 1066 (the earth is a flat bowl at the centre of the universe) or the 1850s (travelling at speeds greater than thirty miles per hour will cause you to die of suffocation). In the late 1800s the British Parliament debated a bill to close the patent office because *everything had been invented!* Each generation of the human race has basked in its own cocoon of smugness, only to be shattered in its turn.

What scientists really think

We have scientists to do what witch doctors and then ministers of religion used to do — to tell us what is going on! As we've hinted at above, though, while ordinary people believe in science, many scientists don't! There is a subject taught at universities around the world, called epistemology, which is 'the science of science'. It is usually only taught to final year science students, (perhaps because it tends to disturb people!) and can be summed up in two basic tenets:

1   That almost everything we now believe about the world will sooner or later end up being superceded. This has always proven to be the case in the past, and there is no reason to think it will

be otherwise in the future. (You need have no doubt at all that in 200 years some of our most dearly held givens of reality will be smiled at by school children — if schools, or children, still exist!)

2   Real advances in understanding (either about yourself or in the scientific domain) don't just add on bit by bit to our existing knowledge, instead new research data periodically forces a complete shake-up of the whole damn thing. The evidence necessitates a totally new picture to be drawn from scratch. Scientists eventually get used to this. In personal life, it is the same. Your understanding of life, if you stay open to it, will be one long series of complete updates. (You will remember times in your life to date when this has happened, when some event or experience simply changed everything, for ever.) On the day you die you will still be revising your view of reality.

So understanding is always transitory. An initial reaction to this discovery is to feel disorientated. If we're bound to be wrong eventually, why try to understand anything? But this realisation is the beginning of freedom. When you start to accept that all we can ever do is make working guesses at what is real and true, then you begin to rely on some new tools in your day-to-day mental life: imagination, playfulness, *joie de vivre*, a kind of 'Well, it all doesn't make (much) sense (yet), but it's a beautiful puzzle, and what the heck, may as well be happy'.

Whether you are a scientist or philosopher, or 'just' trying to understand your wife or husband, or get through to your three-year-old or teenager, you mustn't back off when you don't succeed all at once. Life is a puzzle! Have a go, and see what happens. You can respect, and like, and get along with someone, without ever having them 'figured out'. Or you may have them figured out one day, and have to start all over again the next. It's important not to be too 'serious' about such things.

This does not mean letting go of thoughtfulness or care. These are the intensifiers of our connection to life. Reality may be a fleeting ghost, but right now it is here, palpably 'real', and we should engage with it fully. This kind of balancing act — to invest totally in life, knowing all the time you can never have it all figured out — takes guts. Or to put it another way, it takes love.

We know more than we can ever hold in our thoughts at one time
We love more than we can ever understand
And still there is so much more of life just
waiting to be loved.

Loving is the only real encompassing way to approach the mystery of the universe — with a mixture of awe, gratitude, and curiosity. Loving the physical world, the world of beauty, art and nature, is a step that many have reached. The next step, a loving attitude towards *oneself* and other *people* (the subject of this book), is a greater challenge. It is a big thing to totally open yourself and your heart to another single separate being whom you cannot possess or control, and whose very life may one day flicker out like a candle before your eyes. Because of the insecurity of our childhoods, we so much want to grasp and to hold, to analyse and explain. 'That's a beautiful painting. I must have it.' But have you noticed that the beauty is never quite as great again? Luckily there are visions of such beauty and glory in the world that even our possessiveness just fades away. It is enough to have seen them. So it is with relationships, and with life itself. It's enough to have been there.

So let's end the philosophy class! We often start out in life wanting to possess and control. Next we want to understand. Eventually we reach the higher stage, where we want only to live in love. We stop chasing the butterfly and it settles on our sleeve.

The fact that you are reading this book means you have reached this higher stage. Consciously or not, you've decided to go after the big one. Congratulations! Now we can start on the details.

The experience of love

Any attempt to describe or define love comes back to a reminder of something that you already know. That state of grace, transcendence, simple happiness in being here for a time on this dazzling planet, has been at least glimpsed by everyone alive. Even loneliness and heartbreak, or the deepest cynicism reflect a knowledge that there is something missing, and that therefore something special must exist.

We can't give love to you but we can tell you how to catch it! Love isn't a hole you fall in, or a fever of the brain! Love arises when the circumstances are right. Our part is to master the art of 'creating a space' for such feelings to arise in. Love is a flame. Accidentally we discover it, it catches us by surprise. Later we learn to tend and feed the flame. The craft of loving, be it tenderness with children, or eroticism with a partner, has always been with the human race, passed along through our history. Today, in the face of the nuclear threat, and our culture's tendency to be hypnotised by violence and carnage, there is a great urgency in continually affirming its existence. Like our ancestors facing the Ice Age, there is no point in staring helplessly at the blizzards and ice. We must turn towards the warmth, and direct our efforts to making it flourish first in our families, and then in the world.

Five Secrets of the Sex-Romance Alliance

Romantic love is a challenge. Most people experience romance for a time, and more often than not, lose it again. Perhaps that's in the nature of romance itself. It cannot be held still or guaranteed, it cannot be pinned down. Writing about love is difficult. Love is a right-brain perception, and words are a left-brain logical way to communicate. That's why music and dance express it better. But words can at least hint at what is there, and lead you to the edge of making your own connections. This is what we will try to do. There are four primary guidelines for capturing romance, the particular kind of love that is appropriate between lifelong partners. They are as follows:

1   Romance is definitely about sex.

2   Romance means treating your lover as a stranger.

3   Romance means giving up control, but not submission.

4   Romance means noticing the beauty.

5   Romance means being constantly connected.

Now let's expand.

Romance is definitely about sex

In the bad old days, romance was what women craved, and men did not understand or even believe in. Many, perhaps most, marriages foundered on this startling lack of common ground. Mid-twentieth century man's acute lack of timing, finesse, sense of atmosphere, slowly turned his wife off intimacy and sexuality, even from affection. But it was rarely all his fault. His partner's lack of self-esteem, her unassertiveness, her unwillingness to stylishly demand and seduce and delay and surrender would equally play their part in letting romance fall away.

This dual inadequacy led her to miss out on the romance and physical satisfaction that she needed, while making him feel boorish and unwanted, or aggressive and desperate (sometimes both). Most of the time no-one was to blame, it was just an unhappy confusion.

Even those who took pride in themselves as being 'skilled' lovers, actually mistook romance for its Hollywood trappings: roses, chocolates, expensive dinners and silk sheets! (It's revealing to hear women talk and joke about men's endeavours in this regard.) The ploy works, and has thus become time-honoured, in as much as the lady may well surrender. But she does so from a point of view of 'Well, at least he's trying!' rather than any deep merging of souls. 'Trappings' are valuable sometimes because they invite a sense of luxuriance and care, and therefore relaxation, which encourages love to emerge, but the externals never make up for real contact, which can just as likely happen in a tent in the rain! Romance is an interpersonal skill that goes beyond spending $100 or $10 000!

Twentieth century man has special trouble in this area because our biology plus our culture creates an inbuilt contradiction. Men and women are different, but our culture took what was an exciting contrast and made it into an almost unbridgeable rift. To reconnect our sexuality and our emotional needs with those of our partners, a whole generation has had to take an unprecedented step. We've had to learn to talk to each other!

The pattern of female sexuality is so different from the male pattern that at first glance it looks like bad design. In the animal kingdom females seem to 'tolerate' intercourse, which is brief, and limited to fixed 'seasons'. There is enormous variety in animal sex, from tortoises which go right on eating, to birds which grow special feathers and spend half a year in sex-oriented display and courtship, to female spiders who at the height of copulation eat their male right up (now there's a climax for you!). However no female animal species are orgasmic, and they have no need to be, for this has little connection with fertility. Human females on the other hand, are capable of having profound, sweeping orgasms, which can go on for some time. Women, however, need more time to become aroused, and respond to very different cues in arriving at this state.

The male sexual pattern — arousal, pleasure, release — was so obvious, rapid and easily arrived at that it was long seen as the norm. Female sexuality, at least of the passionate, playful, pleasure-seeking kind, was so unexplored that the Victorian era could construct a widely accepted myth of its non-existence. While mocking the Victorians, we live in their shadow, and many older women today (who know differently in their mind) still find difficulty in re-educating their body to a level of erotic pleasure which is normal and health giving.

'Behavioural' sex therapy techniques which tend to treat sexual dysfunction by applying male methods to women encouraging them to masturbate, relax, become desensitised and so on meet with only mixed success. These work well with good, caring therapists, and where a couple are basically loving towards each other already, but when trust and communication are damaged, such techniques fail totally and can leave the couple feeling *really* defective. There has been more success in using 'female' methods to treat men. Both impotence and premature ejaculation respond well to a method called 'sensate focus' whereby couples must learn to massage and pleasure each other in turn in non-sexual ways, in order to regain a sense of pleasure and lovingness that de-emphasises 'performance', and to educate their bodies to allow more overall pleasure and relaxation.

The pleasure of the chase

Our culture over-exaggerated our natural male/female differences, and sexual compatibility problems arose as a result. Nature hardly intended males and females to be incompatible! There is a unique way that male and female sexuality, although so different, are meant to combine. It lies in the dance between male urgency, and

THE PLEASURE OF THE CHASE

female delay, between seductiveness and backing off, between pursuit and 'surrender'.

One of our couple workshops burst into hilarity recently when someone mentioned an experience shared by almost every couple present — the 'Bathroom Groping Syndrome'. The unsuspecting husband, going into the bathroom to get his socks, finds his wife naked, stepping out of the shower. The sight of all this delicious flesh moves him to grope and grab, affectionately but without warning. She feeling not at all sexy, shrieks and leaps away. Cold hands don't help! Well, it was worth a try. For most couples this is just a bit of a giggle, but it can also be a metaphor for how things go right or wrong in the bedroom — the whole issue of timing and making real contact.

A man needs to be confident in his pursuit, confident enough to overcome setbacks and delays, some of which are just part of the game. A woman needs to be confident in her attractiveness, in her right to wait for just the right conditions, so that she may share in full sensual release. Both learn that sex is a game of chaser and chaste, hide and seek, seduction and surrender. The 'technique' of lovemaking begins with simply being childlike and easy going. Love is playful, it's as simple as that. This is why most pornographic films are such a failure — people being serious about sex just look silly. Lovers are like little children — giggling, teasing, chasing and being free and unfettered. The tease and retreat, chase and rebuff, the surprise acquiescence cycle recurs over and over. While it feels like play, an ancient pattern is taking place, which builds to an 'unbearable' tension. Despite fantasies to the contrary, a man would find a passively acquiescent partner very unsatisfying. And as some women know, being one is equally a drag. Getting there is all the fun. The game intensifies, develops urgency and intensity, but it is never serious, and preferably never predictable.

The greater the build-up, the greater the release. That's the secret.

Why there is courtship

Courtship is of course, the biggest chase of all. Sexual tension accompanies the exploration of personalities, and allows a massive charge to accumulate, which will increase the impact of bonding when it finally occurs.

It's important in the courtship phase, especially for older couples who are experienced in past relationships, to practise some of the 'holding out' that goes with courtship in the young. We've counselled divorced people who, although blasé and disappointed in sex from their marriage experiences, hop into bed immediately with new acquaintances, and although enjoying the recreation and intimacy this brings in a lonely time in their lives, are quickly dissatisfied and move on again. To establish a bond of significance requires some smouldering of sexual tension, so that a unique pattern of attraction and interaction can grow between a courting couple of whatever age. Thus the pair both give their systems time to learn that this person is different, and requires them to be different.

> I slept with a couple of guys in the months just after my marriage broke up, and it was nice, but I knew they were nothing serious. It took a while to admit to myself that I wanted another long-term relationship. Gavin and I slept together soon after we met, but I began to realise that he could mean a lot to me, and strangely, that I wanted to slow it all down. I thought he might get angry that I wanted to be 'old fashioned', but he was surprisingly understanding. Things are going along very nicely now, and I've gained confidence from the fact that he still likes to be around me.

Confidence, being true to yourself, finding the timing that is right for you, are all important parts of being a lover. There is no doubt that technique is important — everywhere in the world folklore praises the skilled lover, male or female. Nonetheless, when you make love, you are a total person, you take to bed your whole personality, of which sexuality is only one part. Consequently sexual technique is only one aspect even of physical love. Where love is present, technique may even be unnecessary. Good communication will make a skilled lover out of a novice. Which brings us to the next step.

Romance means treating your lover as a stranger

Let's say you are already with someone, either in a recent, or a long-standing relationship. You spend time together, and time apart. When you come together at the end of the day, it is important to recognise that *you are not meeting the same person*. This is critical. No-one is ever the same person, even from second to second. The first part of loving is to watch, listen, sense and feel the person who is actually with you at that moment — not a fantasy or a memory of them.

The never-ending story

Part of the complexity of relationships is that people continually unfold. As one part of our make-up clarifies we change and another layer can emerge. By analogy, our body changes too, our skin constantly shedding, our bones taking up new calcium, our organs replacing themselves completely in a matter of months with new cells. We are constantly and fundamentally being rebuilt. We are like a river which is still there, though the water moves on. All the matter on earth swirls and recombines in such myriad ways, somewhere in your body is an atom, or an electron, that was part of Jesus Christ's body, and also of Genghis Khan's!

Since our partner is constantly changing, relating becomes a continual and endless dialogue between two people who are never the same from one moment to the next, whom we simply have to get to know all over again if we are to stay in real contact. The change is gentle, but continual.

Think about how you approach a total stranger that you must deal with for some reason. You act with courtesy, with tentative unknowing, using your senses fully to apprehend how they are unique and how to meet them appropriately. By contrast, someone we have lived with for years we may now treat with incredible rudeness through sheer habit, for instance in areas like privacy, or in giving unasked-for advice and criticism. Try treating your partner (or your children) for one day with the same courtesy you'd give the person in the corner shop.

Expecting your partner to be the same person from day to day can actually create blockages, and lead bad expectations to come true. A friend told us of this as follows:

> It's getting close to bedtime. I've been feeling all day that I want to have sex tonight. I find in my thoughts during the evening that I am judging Gail as either good (conforming to my hopes for a responsive, 'sexy' partner) or bad (not conforming to these hopes). My responses to her are affected by my guesses about how she feels towards me. If she is uncertain, not playing a comfortable mirror image to my wants, then I feel hostile. I respond critically to any sign of her non-conforming with my hopes (for instance a neutral comment like 'Gee, I'm tired') so that she, sensing an atmosphere of non-acceptance, begins to tense up and withdraw. My program

of 'I want sex and I expect/fear that I won't get it' leads to the disruption of intimacy. A situation that once held many possibilities is now frozen into only one.

As partners we often become so adjusted to each other that patterns can be acted out with nothing ever being said. A casual observer might be totally mystified by many couple exchanges. For instance, a whole lifetime's sexual contracts can be covertly made by discussing what TV shows to watch!

'There's nothing much good on tonight' *(except you sweetheart!)*
'No, there isn't is there!' *(grin!)*

or alternatively . . .

'Coming to bed?' *(Wanna . . . you know . . .?)*
'I think I'll watch the movie.' *(Not tonight Josephine.)*
'Haven't you seen it before? . . . It goes pretty late.' *(You never want to any more . . .)*

and so on.

Another set of problems arise if, by contrast, a partner wants to act 'helpful', like a kind of sexual social worker.

Sometimes she will 'act' sexy but I know it isn't for real. I go along with this, and sometimes it's fine, but other times I don't really enjoy it, I feel very patronised. I feel like I am a child instead of being a desirable man.

Faking sexual interest and response is a disastrous step. Sexual penetration without emotional involvement is especially self-destructive. It is so hard to tell a lie with one's body, and so fundamentally dishonest with one's loved one. It is pitiful to read now the women's magazines of the 1950s and 1960s, with their ads for girdles, vaginal deodorant sprays, and the ubiquitous KY Jelly, to help nature along! It's fashionable now to minimise the sexual revolution, and the impact of feminism, but looking back, it's clear that (especially in the domain of sexual fulfilment) we have travelled 1000 years in a decade or two.

Sexual penetration — A1 regular, missionary approved — became the be-all-and-end-all of sex. Add to that the 'athletic movement' ethic of sex, with double simultaneous orgasm at any price, and you can understand why people started to wonder if it was worth all the trouble (especially when complicated further by contraceptive needs and constraints). By contrast (we hesitate to say 'on the other hand'!) many couples who we've talked with have found a whole range of sexual touching by a partner, be it aggressive and fully involved, playful, or sleepy and tender, can be just what the situation calls for — not the full involvement of sexual intercourse, but a generous indulgence. After all, you don't starve your partner of food because you aren't quite so hungry. Differing appetites are a myth. They reflect the lack of skill and practice in connecting with and winning one's partner.

Only be who you are, and only do what you feel like doing. When both partners feel accepted and good, then there will be more sex than you know what to do with. A wide range of sharing and giving is available. As a general principle, allow each person his or her own expression, be responsive without feeling pressured, and sex will start to flow and merge with your whole life in a varied and easy way.

Where do you go to my lovely?

The word masturbation (will someone invent a nicer sounding word?) is defined in the dictionary as sexual self-stimulation. Sadly, for an awful lot of couples sex is just this — self-stimulation with the help of someone else's body. One symptom of this is the oft-reported tendency to fantasise another partner than the one you are with. No-one really likes to be treated like a prop in someone else's fantasy. (Shared fantasies, of course, are a different matter.) If you find that you are having this experience of 'having sex', but not making love, then you are probably ready to re-pattern your communication into something more satisfying.

Men and women may need help to just 'be' together. Sexual communication is about feelings and sensations as much as about actions. How much you feel depends on how you occupy your own body. Try this:

1   Right now, notice your right foot. Is it comfortable and warm? When you are noticing this, you are 'feeling'. Go back and do it again. Feeling is different to thinking, which you use to read this sentence. Sexual communication needs a lot more 'feeling' than thinking.

J. WRIGHT

2 Now you can 'feel', see if you can feel the difference between 'open' and 'closed'. For instance, notice the difference between the front of your body, and the back. You will probably find the front is more 'open'—softer, warmer, more relaxed. See if you can make your face muscles and skin and nerves feel 'open', then 'closed', then 'open' again. (If this is hard, imagine you are looking at a hostile stranger, then imagine looking at a photo of a close friend.)

3 Take these new skills to bed! As you lie together talking or gently touching or holding, simply allow yourself to become more and more open. At the same time, let your touching of your partner be the kind that invites his or her body to relax and settle. When they touch you, 'go to meet' the touching by 'being in' that part which is touched so you fully let in the contact being offered. A world of increased joy awaits you.

Hello stranger

For a time in a relationship, people often try hard to 'be' the right kind of person, and act in the ways that will get the reaction they want. Eventually it dawns on them that the only way to go, the only loving way, is to be real.

Listen to this conversation between a counsellor and a man in his early thirties:

> 'I get scared when I start to feel serious about a woman I'm taking out.'
>
> 'How do you deal with that?'
>
> 'Oh, I get critical of her, find fault, or act aloof.'
>
> 'That must really help.'
>
> 'What else can I do?'
>
> 'Did you ever think of being honest?'
>
> 'You mean, tell her I'm serious about her, and that I'm scared?'
>
> 'How would that be?'
>
> 'She might reject me.'
>
> 'For being yourself?'
>
> 'Uh, yeah!'
>
> 'Then you're lucky aren't you?'
>
> 'Whaat?'
>
> 'You've saved yourself months of messing around. If she doesn't like the real you, you're better off knowing that straight off. She's got no taste!'
>
> 'And she might just accept it!'
>
> 'Then you're really getting somewhere'.

So it all starts with a little self-acceptance. To quote a great biblical expression, gird up your loins! Get yourself together. Notice your actual self-sufficiency, your completeness independent of the other person. Sure you have hopes, wishes, even needs, but whatever happens in this relationship you will nonetheless survive, and you are still okay.

The word 'needs' is often used when we are getting overdramatic. All you ever *need* is air, water, shelter, food and touch. Everything else is a 'want'. Let go of childlike delusions: 'I'd fall apart without her'; 'I'd die if he didn't love me!'. Smile at yourself and then abandon all such melodrama.

Conducting a relationship, even holding a conversation, is a matter of reaching inward to yourself and then outward to the other person. Feel what you are feeling, then, if it seems appropriate, talk about what you are feeling and ask for what you want. Do what you want to do, respond to your partner's feelings and requests, and keep moving on in endless dialogue.

Whenever you meet, aim to simply perceive the other person as he or she is, free of judgements. Each time you reconnect — at the end of a busy day apart, on the weekend when you wake up — begin again tentatively, notice their beauty, their differentness, find out from them what their experience is of being here at this time. There may be 'unfinished business' left over from the day that you both need to clear out before you can connect. At other times this can simply be allowed to fall away. Only *be* interested if you *are* interested. Use the geography of your house well. Have chairs which face each other, not just the TV. Some couples keep the bedroom for being close (and sleeping) and never discuss problems of the day once they get to bed. Bedtime rituals may include sitting face-to-face, with a drink, the TV off, quietly reconnecting and finishing the day.

J. WRIGHT

It's good to keep your daytime hassles out of your sex life, but the reverse is not true! Sex starts a long time before bedtime. Friendliness, encouragement, shared pleasure, even tiffs and mock arguments during the day and evening all build a 'charge' between the couple which soon aches to be released. Even arguments and standoffs have a sexual component. Most arguments between males and females have a 'foreplay' quality to them. Nagging wives really just want their henpecked husbands to 'make a stand'! Being aware of this will dramatically change your argument style.

Allow a sexual charge to permeate your practical activities done together (though be gradual about it, or nothing will ever get finished). One group of young women we taught decided to call this phenomenon 'housework foreplay'.

Being home when you get home

The most important times of day are often the hours when we arrive home from work and somehow end up in a scramble of kids, rushed meals and miscommunication between the adults. A ritual which we learned, and which is now practised by many couples, is to get together immediately you or your partner returns home, and sit down with some alcohol to drink, and some food with a protein component, such as cheese, salami, even fruitcake or peanuts. Spend just ten to fifteen minutes settling yourselves down, allowing your breathing and heartbeats to start synchronising, which they will as you just sit, talk and be together. If there are children about they will need to understand that they must not intrude or monopolise. This will mean a definite decision with young children: if they intrude, they will be made to leave the room. Talk about good things rather than who had the worst day. These few minutes will give you a shift of mental state, a fuel-up so that meal preparation will be not done on an empty tank and most importantly, will rejoin your couple unit, so that the evening flows smoothly. Children will benefit from the harmony between their parents, even if it means they have to wait a little. Sometimes simple practices like this can alter the whole nature of your daily life in the direction of smoothness and peace.

Give way when merging

Many couples need to learn how to 'merge'. To simply relax together so that boundaries are softened and diffused. Quietly, easily, you will find that you can just learn to 'be' together. As you move into a peaceful space yourself, it invites peace in the other person. Other couples are 'overmerged', and need to learn how to build charge by separating more emotionally, and deliberately setting up a tension. (Such couples experience each other as comfortable companions, or mates, but feel little sexual charge together, and may be more attracted to strangers instead.)

Remember that attraction is the natural program. All you need do is get out of its way! There are a million ways to be loving. If excitement arises, great, if laughter bubbles out, great. A fight, well, at least it's contact! Sleepiness — you must've needed it. Lust — that's wonderful! But you can't program which it'll be. All we can promise you is that when people stop acting and just be themselves, then love arises in a form that is perfect for here and now.

Romance means giving up control, but not submission

Surrender and win

In the folklore we grew up with — the cartoons, the TV shows, the jokes told at the dinner table, marriage was often portrayed as 'The battle of the sexes'. It was expected that marriage was a power struggle. If the struggle got out of hand, then the marriage broke up. Marriage break-ups were rarer then, so that people whispered of bitterness and pain. It was natural then to go one step further and, in explaining the reasons for a break-up, to cite fighting as the cause. Yet we tend to forget that happy couples fight too. It is not just fighting that causes marriages to founder, but the lack of some ingredient in the way we choose to conduct our fights.

People who fight badly do so for one basic reason — because they are trying to gain *control* over the other person. Happy couples fight too, and have differences, and get exasperated, and may yell and storm around, but they have long since given up on trying to control the other person. Control is the booby prize — what you try to get when you don't trust that your needs will be met any other way. Trying to get love through control is like trying to catch a butterfly with two bricks. By the end of this century there will be available highly realistic android (or robot) lovers, and those who want to will be able to buy 'partners' that will do whatever they wish. Perhaps it will take till then for some people to discover that this is (almost) no fun at all.

It takes faith to realise that in close relationships you get more of what you want when you stop trying to get it. So fight by all means, but do it for different reasons, and expect different results.

From distress to bliss is not so far

There is little separating marital bliss and marital pain. Our work with couples validates our own personal experience — that the changes needed to become happy are actually very simple. Thriving couples have very similar patterns of interaction to 'incompatible' ones, but they simply do not invest these patterns with anything like the same melodrama. They still play games (in Eric Berne's sense), but not desperate games. If you listen to or watch your happier friends with their partners in conversation, there's a basic playfulness and trust that underlies their interactions. This element transforms bickering to flirtation, changes a fight from a life-and-death struggle into energising excitement.

> I visited some friends one weekend, and to begin with I was embarrassed and confused at their interaction. They were arguing at breakfast, but there was something strange about it. The kids just went right on eating, and as my friends carried on the argument, their faces just didn't match their words. In my family, when people argued, they looked cold and terse, and I as a child felt dreadful. This seemed different. Were they fighting or were they making love?

It takes great poise to fight with good humour and to abandon melodrama. The self-sufficiency needed to be able to abandon control in a relationship may come from very early childhood. Perhaps the seeds of good marriage lie in having a security from way back, that frees the adult relationship from infantile dependencies. If that were the case most of us would be doomed! With our less-than-perfect backgrounds, we must learn to negotiate trust and discover our independence from square one. 'When John left me I thought I would just die. Luckily, it was my bowling night.'

Fighting with style

Good fighting takes practice. We often ask the counsellors we train to go and watch a movie called *Man Woman and Child*, which has a stunning fight scene at the climax of the film. A husband and wife have pretended to be happy for years, and are certainly caring and committed, yet somehow the real spark is missing. They have raised two girls, and prospered, but now must deal with the arrival of an illegitimate child from a long-ago infidelity of the husband. They try to be 'reasonable' but finally all the feelings of betrayal and fear pour out. People watching the movie cannot believe that so much anger could be let out (in 'real life'), with no-one getting hit, walking out, or giving up. In two minutes, the fight resolves itself. The couple express anger, and then admit their fears, and then find the beginnings of reassurance. Many people find the fight scene exhilarating to watch. Others can't believe it – it's 'too good to be true'. The sense of disbelief lies in the viewer's own experience of living with mistrust. Few people in real life trust, and fight, as well as this.

Trust isn't a leap in the dark – it comes from gradual, accumulated experience. It is part of courtship (finding out what you've court!). You proceed in steps, noticing in a range of situations, and especially under stress, how your prospective partner reacts, and how you react to him or her. This might sound contrived or cold-hearted, but it isn't, it simply happens along the way. Early in a relationship it's good that you stand on your independence. You hunger for union, but you don't *need* it. Or as teenagers say, 'I'm not *that* desperate'! You can check out important aspects of a person over a time duration long enough to get a real picture.

Trust has simple elements. Does this person keep to his or her word? Do they take responsibility for their actions? Small stuff like that.

A note of caution here. You may have grown up in a family where the adults were untrustworthy to each other, perhaps violent, addicted to alcohol, sexually unfaithful or abusive, dishonest with money and so on. Such patterns lead to a kind of inverted trust, in that you unconsciously feel at home with similar people. In a sense you can trust them to be untrustworthy.

Sometimes people from such backgrounds feel attracted to 'losers' and marry a series of them, at the same time appeasing their commonsense with rationalisations like 'All they need is a good woman' or 'My love will heal them'. The attraction is unconscious, until you recognise the pattern. You may have to ignore your choosing mechanism, for a while, and use your head instead. If you want a partner, you are entitled to a trustworthy, adult one. Don't settle for less.

As courtship proceeds, the experimentation will expand, based on the security already established. You will find yourself voicing small disagreements more often now, so as to establish your freedom and identity within the friendship. Once assured of your own strength (that you will not allow yourself to be 'swallowed up' by the other person) you can begin to make small moves into depending — not because you have to, but because it opens new possibilities. You don't 'fall' in love (boy has that phrase done some damage!). Anything you fall into is bound to be a hole! It's more like a ladder. You step on one rung, carefully, and see where that gets you. If it looks good you move on up. If you want excitement, go quicker, but don't close your eyes.

As your senses give you more and more messages of safety, you begin increasingly to go with the flow, abandoning yourself to the dialogue, to feelings of generosity, coyness, pursuit, allowing the relationship to unfold. Just 'be' together and delight in what happens. Let love make you.

When people seek closeness, it is never possible to know in advance what form this will take. Sometimes what one (or both) wants is purely affection — non-sexual holding and stroking. Be sure to express what you need and, if necessary, what you don't need. Both men and women sometimes want affection that isn't turned into erotic touching. As we mentioned in Chapter 4, you may even figure out how old (young) you're feeling, and from this derive what you are wanting. Perhaps you want to be held safely, to be stroked, or to be just held, read stories to, have your hair tousled, to stay in bed and be brought chicken soup, or whatever!

When you ask for what you want, be direct. Don't 'steal' affection when the other person isn't ready by making a grab, or sidling up when you know the other person isn't responsive. Don't *give* if what you want is to *receive*. A child needs affection to survive. As adults we like and thrive on affection too, but it is no longer a life or death thing. Just because the other person isn't responsive right there and then, don't turn this into a rejection fantasy. Go and do something!

Sexual release is the clearest example of letting go of control in a relationship (and the reason why 'frigidity' and 'impotence' are usually more to do with power problems than sexual ones). Orgasm, if surrendered to fully, affects and is felt by every cell of your body. Learning this degree of surrender takes time. Consider the possibility that you now only feel one tenth of the pleasure and union which sex can bring. Think of the possibilities!

You may find that at the height of lovemaking, if you relax and draw back a little from the urge to push, then lust merges into just pleasure in being inside one another, that cycles of pushing and just-experiencing alternate together. Men who are concerned about the duration of intercourse, about 'going the distance', find that this is no longer an issue. Rather than trying to control oneself, the opposite — relaxation — is what works. Relaxation can be still vigorous and surging, but it is always loose and flowing.

Some people have told us of surprising reactions in the moments during and just after orgasm — being wrenched with sobs and tears, or swept with anger or violent feelings or images. These are simply the baggage that has been carried over, releasing in the safety and relaxation your body now feels. Accept and allow these to move through you and they will give way in turn to melting tenderness.

Tenderness and adoration towards a partner are not an illusion, or a spurious after-effect of lovemaking but simply the true feelings which emerge when you abandon, even fleetingly, your normal defences.

From control to pleasure: lovemaking for men

Most men need to re-learn lovemaking. Full loving requires an active re-awakening of the body. Many men in the past were badly damaged in their sexual responsiveness, in their capacity to feel total body pleasure, and therefore in orgasmic intensity. This has come about through a socialisation process that tends to let men value only genital pleasure, and puts constraints even on this.

Watch male babies and toddlers as they sit, unaware of your

presence, engaged in the most innocent self-eroticism, teasing up proud little erections. They know genitals are something special, and (when older) may need to be taught a little propriety, but above all they need to be allowed free exploration of themselves. Little children (in the freer families of today) kiss and stroke and hug each other, and people they like, with abandon. They know no frightening taboos – know all about penises, and 'gaginas' and tampons, and toilets (and at the same time seem to develop their own feelings of privacy and space), so that sex just never becomes a trauma. Many of us adults though, were not so nurtured. In fact many of us were actively hurt and punished for self-loving, both as little children and again as teenagers. The school dictionary at Steve's school was quite progressive, for it actually had 'masturbation' listed. The definition was limited to two words: 'self abuse'! Not much enlightenment there. Naturally one looked up self-abuse, which was defined as 'masturbation'. Thank God for peer group information!

Unlearning desperate sex

Many men learned in their teens a body pattern of sexual half-release, acquired while masturbating jaw-clenched, body rigid, so as not to be found out. It all seems so unnecessary now. Their parents may well have been doing the same in the next room! Men are often so uptight that their orgasms look and sound painful. Comedian Robin Williams points out that it's no wonder men don't fake orgasms – who would want to look that stupid by choice! (It's one of the reasons children are disturbed and damaged by seeing pornographic videos. People don't look like they are having much fun. Genuinely erotic movies, which are a rarity, would do no harm at all to a child.) In past decades, the teenage boy's body learned a pattern of sexual response as a tense, hurried struggle for release, with a guilty aftermath. In a sense, the average male has a pain fetish. In the extreme form, some unfortunate youngsters make mistaken cross-connections at this time between sex and violence or masochism, with obvious consequences for later life.

You may recall watching the movie Coming Home with Jane Fonda and Jon Voigt. The heroine's army officer husband returns from Vietnam supposedly 'charged up' for lovemaking, which is over in seconds. Soon after she meets another veteran, a paraplegic, played by Voigt, whose slightly embarrassed but tenderly exploratory love scene with Fonda is one of the most beautiful we have ever seen on film.

For a proportion of people today, by the time they are adult and sex finally becomes legitimate, all that remains is a brief shudder of release in men, and a cold tight submission in women, and for both a feeling of 'Ohh . . . is that all there is?' The sexuality of a really alive human being is a noisy business, not easy to keep secret in a thin-walled house or apartment! We city dwelling westerners will have to change either our housing or our sense of propriety to make room for real pleasure.

Western lovers are often confused about tension and relaxation in sex. Even a modern writer like Alex Comfort, in the *Joy of Sex*, writes that lovers vary in preference, some liking tense sex (to the degree of bondage play), others relaxed, languorous sexual intercourse, with its possibility for a total loss of identity and separateness. He advises that people try both, especially if their partner finds the other more right for them. Good enough advice, but tension and pain addicts need to know that they are missing out on a world of contact.

Charging up

The concept of sexual tension is a misnomer. A more useful term is that used by the body therapists — the idea of physical 'charge' accumulated in the body like static in a rubbed object. A tense, contracted person can hold very little charge in his or her body. They easily get tired. They will need strong, blatant stimulation to feel excitation, will soon reach a pressure for release once this excitation is gained, and will rapidly de-excite once orgasm is reached. A relaxed, open body will be more receptive to subtle and diverse stimulation, will charge in slow surges, and will be able to maintain a plateau of pleasure for long periods. Discharge will be powerful, longer in duration, and more total in its extent through the body.

Bioenergetic therapist Julie Henderson, in her unique book *The Lover Within*, provides a series of exercises for developing one's body senses and capacities. A basic and simple exercise is suggested for people wanting to expand their capacity for charge and therefore for pleasure. She suggests that people practise sexually stimulating themselves, in privacy, or with the help of a partner, almost to the point of orgasm, then cease abruptly, taking time to deliberately relax their body. They may then spend an hour (moving about, resting, doing other things) before continuing if they wish, to sexual release, which again can be alone, or with a partner. Those who are habitually very contracted in their body may find this idea unbearable! Try it. The key is in relaxation, in deliberately making room for the higher degree of excitation so that you will progressively find that you can hold more and more charge and become more energised, not just sexually but in other spheres of life too.

This physical skill learned from the exercise can be carried on into actual intercourse to help you completely let go of striving or effort for release and simply focus on the sensations that are already happening, rather than pushing for more. To begin with, wait until that magical moment when you *know* orgasm is about to happen. At this point, relax your body totally, especially being aware of your thighs, buttocks and leg muscles. Most men report that when doing this, they experience a much greater release flowing through their whole body. After a time, begin to activate this relaxing, or self-abandonment, earlier in the lovemaking cycle. Don't go on a program — just experiment when you think of it.

Receiving — love, stimulation, praise — is a skill, a way of using your senses, without using your muscles. Germaine Greer pointed out that receptiveness is really a very active process, like eating. You 'eat' (savour, enjoy) the sensations your partner creates in you. Especially if your partner is normally the passive one, experiment with swapping back and forth the control of movement, so that each has the opportunity to concentrate simply on receiving.

Allow more time and space for massage in sexual play, and for its own sake alone. Massage teaches your body to know what relaxation is. This kind of communication begins to move beyond what words can ever say.

At the height of sexual pleasure, open your eyes, and see each other, and merge totally if you dare. Eventually you will understand why Tantric Yoga treats sex as a meditation, a way to union with God.

The trouble with 'New Women' and 'New Men'

For years women complained about pushy but unfeeling males, saying they were domineering, insensitive, and so on. Fair enough. But a different kind of complaint has arisen in recent years. Many of 'today's men' have been so filled with the need to be considerate and 'supportive' that they back off from the really lustful pursuit and assertiveness that characterises 'animal' male sexuality. We talk with many young women these days who are frustrated by the wimpishness of their men, in bed and out, even though this

kind of softer man was what women for a time thought they wanted. Sensitive, yes, but uncertain and childlike — no! If you're a woman you may need to develop signals that indicate the wish to be ravished, to be 'talked into it' or pursued and decided for. Selfishness is appropriate in relationships, as long as you have a clear stop signal.

It isn't just the 'new' man who is letting down his partner. Beyond the bedroom, and over many years now, men have become less and less self-assured. *The importance of authentic manhood has been dimishing all through the industrial era*. Think about fathers as portrayed in popular culture. In a continuous line from Dagwood to Bill Cosby, men are portrayed as charming, lovable, and *docile*. The media father protests, makes his point, maintains the peace, but he is never quite 'with it'. His wife, children, even his pets get the better of him. The advertising industry, recognising who has the spending power, never makes fun of women any more. The fall guy, the dope, the butt of jokes, is always a man. Since the industrial revolution, the obedient man has been the requirement. The dark side of this is the unbroken tradition of wife beating, and child sexual abuse, symptoms of lack of power, and of power misdirected. *A family needs two partners who are powerful, in their different ways. A surprising number of women we speak to yearn for their men to match their power, to be man enough to balance gentleness with strength, and so invite surrender.*

You can be both selfish and considerate at the same time. You can assert any want you have in a relationship, if you also listen to, and accept, your partner's feedback about his or her wants. Total fulfilment of both partners is part of the design. By developing a more assured approach to sex, and communication as a whole, you will find marked changes not just in the pleasure received and given at the time, but also in your body's condition, relaxation, and energy level overall. Outside the bedroom, by being more confident and clear about the sex you are, and the importance of the role you fill, you will generate as a couple both harmony and excitement.

Romance means noticing the beauty

What you notice is what you get

When Steve was a beginning student of family therapy, his teacher began to show the trainees the many things that happen when a family talks together — the subtly shifted chair as someone sits down, how one child frowns as another speaks, a breath held in sharply when a certain topic is raised and so on. The teacher was a dreadful tease, especially to those who, like Steve, were trained as scientists, and therefore had badly damaged thinking skills. She would tell the class, straight-faced, that at any moment there are 1432 possible things a client can do next. One of our already dismayed class said, 'But that means there are 5000 things a family might do at any moment'. 'Yes', said Virginia, 'but don't worry. If it's important, they'll do it again!'

It's a fact that our environment is enormously complex. Even as you read this book there are hundreds of stimuli around you (both external and internal) to which you could give your attention. We literally make the reality around us by what we choose to notice. If you're hungry, the street you are walking down is all food; if you're randy it's all the opposite sex; if you're depressed it's all futile; if you're 'up' it's sunshine and sparkle.

This phenomenon is even more the case with the people we have around us. Let's imagine that you are angry about something. You may not even know what. Perhaps you have had too many interruptions in your day, or there is a good film you don't have time to see, or someone has made a dumb comment. Or if you are not angry, that you are lonely and feeling left out of things. Whatever the reason, you are not having a good day. Your partner comes home, and says fifteen different things in the first half hour. Four are neutral, ten are positive, one is arguable (crabby, critical, negative). You pick on the arguable part, and start a fight. You have to go carefully because it has to look like *their fault*! Eventually they do fight with you, and (there!) you've proven what a rat they are. Now you can let your anger out with justification. Or if anger isn't your thing, you can get upset, and then you get comforted, and this proves they do love you after all. It ends well, but what a way to get there.

Noticing what you allow your senses to focus on, feel, and hear, is very largely determined by choice, and in fact by habit. You'll recognise this, for instance, in someone who on a sunny day talks about how the farmers need rain, or in yourself when you wonder how long you can feel this happy! Many people we teach will initially be so ill at ease with the relaxation and pleasure they are learning to experience that they will race back to horror stories from the newspaper, or develop the conversation into cynical realms, so that they can once again feel comfortably depressed. We just tease them mercilessly and they soon relinquish the habit. Don't be fooled by pretend intellectual positions like 'What right have you to be happy in a world like this?'. The universe is gloriously neutral. Feelings are fickle so you may as well choose those feelings which empower and enhance your life and your actions. The doers of this world, who solve problems, invent remedies, and organise a better world for us all, are steadily optimistic, one foot forward for the demonstrable progress of the human race, one eye on the way ahead.

Meanwhile, let us return to the family. The rule is simple: whatever you pay attention to in your partner, or your children, that quality will grow and increase. Every partner is both beautiful and ugly. Every child is a genius and a dill. It depends on you. Notice and attend to what you like to experience, and watch it manifest.

It helps if you comment.

'Gee it's great to talk to you like this. We haven't done this for ages.'

It will then be much more likely that your partner will say something like *'Thanks. It's good for me too!'*.

Similarly you can show your partner or children what you like by smiling, touching them, going and standing with them, being affectionate and expressive in a casual way as well as the more intensive exchanges. Very slight and casual validations of what you like will often be the most effective.

When people have an expectation of the negative, and selectively respond to this, they can make it happen. Sometimes people make major life choices (like choice of spouse or job or how many children) to fulfil a negative expectation of life.

The power of expectation applies even to physical health. In your body there are sure to be aches and pains present, right now, if you look for them. But if you look right now for pleasure, for warmth, for relaxed places in your body, there they are, there they will always be. Stay with these for longer, feel them grow.

Develop a habit of pleasuring yourself in this way. Notice the beauty in your partners, how they look, their moves, what they say and do. Be aware of how magical your children are. How well behaved they occasionally can be! You can comment on it if you wish, but noticing and appreciating is really all you need to do. Do this and it will change your family and your world.

Romance means being constantly connected

Make your contacts electric

There's a great symmetry in relationships. You get exactly what you give. Some men spend a day hidden behind a newspaper, at work, or in the garden shed, then as bedtime approaches, feel a sudden need to be close. They define this purely in sexual terms, and wonder why their spouse doesn't positively light up!

Being in a relationship with another person is quite the opposite of the above. Romance is a kind of continual dialogue, an endless (and endlessly interesting) conversation. Cleaning the house, phoning during the day, caring for babies together, eating dinner quietly, can all be permeated with an air of courtship, a slow build-up, a quick or infinitely understated tension that provides both interest, and at the same time security. The 1950s marriage manuals with their 'ten minutes foreplay' become ridiculous. All of life is foreplay (and after-play, and during-play).

Real contact is not just the rubbing of skin. You can shake one person's hand and the feeling is electric, yet another's hands feel like a wet fish! You can have sex with someone, the most intimate physical contact possible, and yet emotionally not even be present. You can make love from fifty feet away across a crowded room. To be able to project this contact, and yet to do so respectfully, responsively, is the key to romantic connection.

Patrick, a friend of ours, wrote this very honest description of how he overcame a contact problem:

Most of the time Marion and I got on okay, but sometimes this kind of behaviour pattern took over, which was my fault completely. I wanted her to be more affectionate, and I would kind of cling to her, or try to. I knew I was doing it, and what a drag it was to her, but it just made me do it more. She got turned off, and irritated, and I alternately sulked or made rushes at her. Through counselling, I realised that I had been very unsure of myself when younger, and failed at a couple of relationships in my late teens, in just this kind of way. My counsellor asked me to fantasise 'me now', moderately successful and in my thirties, going back to those old relationships, and what I would do. In one instance I imagined that I wouldn't even want the girl who had rejected me! In the other, I imagined myself winning the affection of the woman, four years older than me at the time, with my age and experience. It was a little hilarious, but struck many chords. Back home it seemed very simple. Me liking myself made it easy for Marion to like me. And if she didn't — tough!

Couples nearly always refer to an ebb and flow of contact, which they are aware of from day to day. Those who are comfortable with this recognise that this is the very nature of love, the way it renews itself. Women and men who are literally 'in love' in this way seem to glow from it. It's not just that they are having good sex, but that their whole life has an energy source that is constantly polarising, building energy, discharging it like lightning to the earth, only to recharge all over again. Experienced couples find out either by thought and discussion, or by good luck, that a cyclic relationship maximises shared pleasure. Perhaps this is the most fundamental dynamic of sex — that a little frustration actually heightens pleasure and bonding*. The higher the mountain, the longer the climb, the better the view. Time and travel away from each other actually helps the process for some couples. The moods of the menstrual cycle become part of this rise and fall, as do the longer cycles of life — the passage of children into one's life and out again, even our own aging process and the changes this brings. Remember Henry Fonda and Katherine Hepburn in *On Golden Pond*. The surface abrasiveness between them seemed to thinly veil a strong, slow lifetime passion.

---

* This can be overdone, as in the addiction to sexual 'conquests' which some men (and women) become trapped in. They've not discovered how to build and accumulate sexual excitement except through the strangeness of a new partner. It's the chase that excites them, and they will pursue you ardently, but once you're conquered they lose all interest.

Romantic attraction builds from waiting; from holding out for the right time and circumstances, and for trust to grow. It's the difference between a popsong and a symphony (and both can be great). Old people will tell you about the incredible excitement that went with long courtships, with eagerly awaited consummation (a lovely word). By contrast many kids we talk to, especially young women, are bored and disappointed with sex by the time they're fifteen.

It's the strong connections that make possible really powerful turbulence. While variety is an essential part of life, this does not seem to be satisfied by varying one's partners. People who change partners in rapid succession almost always experience the paradoxical effect that it all becomes the same. People who are monogamous (have one partner) and are still *experiencing* each other rather than going through the motions, find that paradoxically their lover is never the same — that extraordinary variety begins to develop! We'd like to make it a bumper sticker, but can't quite fit it in: *Be monogamous and sleep with a new person every night!*

Monogamy: Where you can really play around

Because of the trust involved in allowing such deep access to your being, it is not possible to be involved sexually with more than one partner and expect anything but confusion. We've become more and more preachy on this account, from the sheer weight of our clients' experience. Adultery is a sure path to pain, an attempt to isolate yourself from hurt by farming out your emotional life into safe compartments for head, heart, body and spirit. The result is simply that no part of your life is ever complete.

Wouldn't it be revolutionary if people began to acknowledge that it might take a few decades to really get to know another person? When our parents' generation talked about working at marriage, they so often meant 'bearing your cross' — in other words submitting. But what if a relationship actually does take time and effort? Would it be worth having a go?

Total commitment — when you find the person (or cause, or vocation) worthy of it — is the biggest adventure in life. It is the highest mountain with the best view. In long-term partnership what develops through exploration is a sense of connection that overrides distance and time. You can begin to feel the other's heartbeat and emotions alongside your own, like soft waves washing over you. You feel both clearly separate, and gently merged, from moment to moment, as it suits. The actual time duration of this relationship may be long or short, but it feels and, for all we know, may be, eternal.

Love in perspective

Long term commitment between a man and a woman is a specific and advanced form of loving, yet one to which many people aspire. The name we give this variety of love is 'romance'. Romance is not the ultimate love or the centre of our life's efforts. We are surrounded by friends, children, work and nature. It's appropriate to spread our love around. Nonetheless romance is a major source of human joy and security — a skill worth pursuing. One day each of us will be alone again, but in the years between we will seek intimacy, and finding it will want to deepen it. It we are successful even momentarily in our primary pair relationship then we will generate an energy that spreads out into the world around us. Life will be enhanced.

Some people will give up this search, or find another equally beautiful way to direct their life force. But living with romance has a unique glory, and we wish you well if you choose to take the chance.

CHAPTER 6

Advanced Lessons

You are here on this planet to learn to love.
And that's all.

She: (thinks)	*Will I start writing the world's greatest novel, or will I change the baby's nappy?*	
He:	*What's that awful smell?*	
She:	*It was a dark and stormy night . . .*	
He:	*Huh?*	

Why Do We Do Things?

Why get out of bed in the morning? Why take a holiday? Why spend twenty years raising children?

You often do the right thing without knowing why. Getting married and having kids is no exception to this. Sometimes though, we can lose our way, and at these times it helps to stop and go back to our basic reasons. What are we really doing here?

If you think about it, the answer to human motivation is quite simple. We do what we do because it makes us feel good. Outward acts are always done for internal goals. From going surfing, to saving the world, it's no different — we pursue a feeling of rightness and flowing connection. Even violent and final actions are still aimed at finding some inner peace at last.

Dear Mary,
I just couldn't take it any longer. I have tried and tried, but the
torment is just too great. I have taken the only course of action left
to me. I have sold the canary. See you tonight,

John

The paradox of doing what makes us feel good is that strangely,
it does not necessarily lead to greediness, or sloth, or callousness
to others. These are only the fate of those people who are
exceptionally unskilled in their selfishness. That's why these
destructive attributes, though they have always been present in
the world, never really predominate. What makes us feel good,
ultimately, goes beyond simple gratification.

Selfishness pays

A friend of ours, we'll call him Ross, came into some money —
royalties for some writing work he had done years before. This
was around Christmas 1985. He was sitting watching TV with his
baby son on his knee, when the first film of the Ethiopian famine
came onto the screen. He thought about it for a moment or two
and then wrote a cheque for the full sum he had received, and
posted it to a development agency he knew would use it well. (It
was an act of spontaneous, but considered generosity that was
being repeated many times over around the world.) He told us
later that every time Ethiopia was mentioned in the news after that
he felt positive, he had done something. Significantly to him, the
film clip had shown *parents*, holding their babies just like he was
holding his, and he had simply felt the connection. Feeding them
was just like feeding his own child.

When you were a youngster, probably like us you were told
that selfishness was something you had to fight against. Perhaps
though, all we need really do is make our selfishness more effective.
Ross watched his TV news with the informed heart of a parent,
and his 'selfish' gratification came from feeding people. Our needs
seem to move ever upwards. We are programmed towards
behaviour which is more and more integrated, more and more
'right'. Have you ever watched young kittens playing endlessly,
chasing, rolling, exploring their world? A kitten's internal program

is, through play, to become a superbly co-ordinated hunter. As a kitten grows into an adult cat, it gradually ceases playing, becomes more sedate. Humans have a program to learn. We never cease our exploration. Even when fed, housed, loved and valued, we still pursue self-realisation, union with life, *something more.*

Human actions in the world only make sense when we realise this push for personal transcendence. The urge is to have one's beliefs, knowledge, emotions and actions all finally moving together in synergy. Occasionally, fleetingly, you reach such a state, and it makes you want more.

The concept of ourselves as seekers of truth has all but been lost in modern life. It's hardly the view of man you are presented with daily in the media. The daily 'news' presents us, in vivid and unnecessary detail, with the tiny proportion of places where the human race is going wrong. Imagine if the news were governed by a sense of proportion: *'Here is the news. Four billion people today got fed, co-operated with each other, and were really nice to their children. A few slipped up, but nothing worth mentioning. And now on to the weather . . .'.*

It's no wonder our world view is badly askew. Similarly our childhood teaching is negative, our potential is undersold. Were you told in childhood that enlightenment was to be your purpose? Or did your parents just tell you to stay out of trouble? All the evidence points to us having a higher nature, which in spite of being lost, confused, and as good as destroyed over and again, reasserts itself as reliably as life itself.

Programmed to be good?

It's in the very difficulties of living that our positive nature is evident. Some years ago Steve worked on a healing program for Vietnam veterans. Among the many stories he listened to, one stands out. One ex-soldier had suffered stress reactions and personality problems over fifteen years, triggered by a single incident in Vietnam, which eventually he talked about, and to which he began to become reconciled. He had, in the course of a whole tour of duty, only shot once at a visible target. On a jungle path he had come face-to-face with a North Vietnamese soldier. Both men raised their weapons, but our friend shot first. He then stood numbly, as his patrol rushed forward. After the all clear, the others routinely searched the enemy soldier's body, and found letters and photos from the dead man's young family. Looking at these mementoes an awareness of the enormity of killing swept over him, and he became numb with shock. He was, in his own words, 'useless' for the rest of the war.

Think about this. A soldier, trained and employed to kill people, kills one man to save his own life, and is shattered by the experience. Does this fit your stereotype of young soldiers? Our work with the veterans of a number of wars, and the research we have read, indicates that this aversion to killing is more the rule than the exception. Perhaps we've all been mesmerised by the media into a paranoid world view? Are people better than we think?

Finding the beauty inside

Robert Carkhuff said 'We are born with only the *potential* to be human'. Many people are now aware of this potential — pursuing it in their lives and deliberately fostering humaneness in their children. People raised with love become strong yet self-regulating, non-conforming yet co-operative, idealistic and yet practical. They make a difference in the world.

We all want to *feel* right, and so we strive to *do* right. All of our passions, even our guilt and confusion, stem from this. The world outside us has meaning only as the grist for our individual and collective salvation. Our actions in the world are simply aimed at producing internal balance. If we see a beautiful work of art, or hear glorious music, we feel its beauty reflected in us and our spirit soars. The beauty however is *in us*. A painting does not have beauty, hanging alone in a gallery, unless we are there to see it.

We live through the material world, including the people around us. We want to feel beautiful inside, so we seek it outside. We want to feel peaceful, so we seek to build a peaceful world. And since the dual fate of western man has been to feel both damaged and cut off from the flow of life, we especially need to heal and to feel connected. The externals — family, hobbies, work, our community and even global concerns — are all just the tools with which we anneal our own spirit.

A couple of years ago our friend's house burnt down. We were distraught on his behalf. He had built it himself, a beautiful native timber cottage of great craftsmanship. He wasn't worried at all. He'd enjoyed building it, and was getting a little bored anyway now it was finished. He had some great ideas for the next one!

What Matters?

As you realise that all you are ever working on is yourself, a certain lack of seriousness creeps into one's feelings towards the world. A common error at this point is to become cynical. Cynicism is intellectualised sulking — things aren't perfect, and *it's not fair*! It's vital to let go of this and move on — what can you make out of this glorious imperfection?

What you discover is that value comes from the meaning you *choose* to give to things. You *let things matter*. Even something huge, like the life of your child, only matters because you choose for it to matter. Or put another way, *nothing matters any more than anything else*. On the same day, a Down's syndrome child makes a finger-painting, and a world leader signs a peace treaty. The child may be reaching a peak of personal joy and contribution, the world leader may be badly underachieving! Only they, and no-one else, will ever know.

It's in our family life cycle that the importance of 'making an investment' becomes clearest. From early childhood we have a need to be healed, to feel connected and alive. In our teens we work towards some kind of identity and separateness in ourselves. Still only half formed, we start the process of building intimacy with a partner. Not long after, we find ourselves painstakingly stumbling along through parenthood.

All the time, we are making meaning, we are making life, we are making love.

As we do this, a sense of greater certainty begins to emerge, a sense not only of fulfilment, but of a kind of heroism in what we are doing. We are close to being on the right track.

What, Me a Hero?

Consider for a moment if as a young person you had wanted to become a hero or heroine (and who hasn't at some stage?). What are the options you can take?

1 You could get involved in a war. Once this was a reliable path to glory. You need only take some incredible risk at the right moment, and you would either get killed or be a hero. But war is going right out of fashion.

2 Perhaps you could rescue someone from an emergency. Again the criteria are that you disregard your own health and safety. But it's hard to be there at the right time. You could wander about for years waiting for someone to rescue.

3 You could practise until you are incredibly good at some game where a small ball is knocked about. This is known as sport, and a highly respected, well paid and safe kind of heroism.

4 You could find some way of making vast sums of money. Especially if there is no apparent effort involved, this is a guaranteed path to national respect and recognition.

We have strange heroes.

What, then, do we make of a young mother who wakens seven times in a night to soothe a sick, cantankerous baby, and has done this every night for weeks. Even on the seventh awakening, reeling with fatigue, she is still gentle, caring and patient with the child. This kind of heroine gets no medals, in fact probably draws the odd sneer next day if she fumbles her change at the shop, or looks less than immaculate walking down the street.

Equally unsung is the young father who spends long days in a job he hates, simply to earn the basics of life for his family. He returns home each night, and starts to help out with the children, to paint rooms, dig gardens, fix cars and generally see to his family's welfare. The idea that men are somehow less devoted than women to family and home has been a myth that does great disservice. This is everyday heroism that should never be discounted.

While the media and our own general negativity have led us to think otherwise, the truth is that most men and women, most of the time throughout our history, have been devoted and valiant in the pursuit of a better life for their famillies. Not all their actions were right and not all their priorities were the best ones (and we have no wish to glorify struggle or hardship for their own sakes), but as professionals who work with families, our personal bias is clear — we know who the real heroes are, and what is real achievement. We'd like to see some statues to the unknown parent!

IN MEMORY OF ALL THOSE PARENTS WHO FOUGHT DOMESTIC BATTLES, BROUGHT UP CHILDREN AND LAID DOWN THEIR LIVES FOR THEIR FAMILY.

J. WRIGHT

Small is Powerful

Throughout this book we have focussed on the microcosm — the world which is immediate and personal. However, in the kind of world we live in today, concentrating your energies on your own family, may seem like sticking your head in the sand! People we meet often voice concern about global problems, three of which occur again and again in conversations. These are the degradation of the natural world, the virtual genocide-by-neglect of the world's poor, and the ever-present threat of nuclear war. Our lives are greatly affected, even threatened, by large scale forces which we cannot ignore. These are not remote threats — they are having a documented negative effect on family life right now. Children and teenagers talk about their fear of dying young. Single adults often seem determined to lose themselves in pleasure seeking — the 'yuppie' syndrome. In the meantime parents, who have a greater investment in the future, simply feel a deep and ongoing distress. (It is the role of parents to protect children, but how do we protect them from such huge and faceless threats?)

We must analyse in order to know where to start. There is a sequence on which our human world is built, and its order is probably immutable. The sequence is simply stated: personal peace leads to family peace, which in turn leads to world peace. Each is the foundation of the next. Without at least some personal peace in each individual, neither family or world peace is possible. Without a core of sane and healthy families, society would not last a single generation. To heal our society, then, we must start from the ground up.

Remember our friend mentioned earlier, who financed a couple of small wells in Ethiopia? Each well cost about the price of a good stereo. He did not need to fix the world — it makes a great difference just to feel 'part of the solution'. It is a dangerous mistake to set aside one's own development and the nurturance of relationships, in order to tackle 'more important' concerns. After all, Adolf Hitler wanted to improve the world too. To do good in the world one needs not only good intentions, but to also have one's acts based in personal sanity.

Is this balance possible — to nurture oneself, live a fulfilled and serene family life and yet be an activist in the world? We think this not just possible, but perhaps the only way that works. The world has had many revolutions, but so little real change. Enduring progress can only be made by changing the hearts of individual people. And this is happening. Out of the confusion of ideologies, politics and dogma, the world has come to a very simple turning point. We live or die. And thankfully, in large numbers, people are finally learning to choose life.

Ordinary people, more clearly and articulately, day by day, are expressing what kind of world they want. They want an economic order which tries to be fair. They want natural beauty left in the world and freedom from toxicity in their air, water and food. They want a more human urban landscape. They abhor the cost and danger, even the *idea* of the arms race. This process has spawned leaders quite different from conventional politicians (think of musician Bob Geldof or conservationist Dr Bob Brown). These people emerge suddenly, even reluctantly, and tap extraordinary power, simply because they give voice to what everyone is feeling in their hearts. Their power comes from ordinary people who want the world to be good enough to raise families in.

You're doing it now

So what do *you* do? At one time, you probably saw yourself as an innocent but endangered bystander, and felt totally powerless. Nothing could be less true. Each of the world's core problems stems from a basic problem in people's hearts. The degradation of the earth reflects not our needs but our lack of ability to find real fulfilment, which leads us in turn to greediness and waste. Likewise, it's the lack of inner security that makes us project our hostility onto others, so that we allow the politicians and arms sellers to collectively arm us to the teeth. And finally, it is the lack of personal connection to life that makes the earth's forests, oceans and wild lands seem just a commodity to be exploited.

The state of the earth simply reflects the total of personal consciousness of our five billion souls. So the answer is in our hands. Emotionally secure, sexually fulfilled couples raising bright, alive, self-loving children are a large part of the answer to nuclear war, to economic injustice, to a poisoned environment. By all means become an activist — there has never been greater work to be done, and this will actually help you and your family's mental health. (Research has shown this. Children whose parents are involved in activist organisations addressing world issues are measurably less anxious and depressed. The world may be amiss, but Mum and Dad are doing something about it.)

In wanting to affect the world, don't ever become a *hyper*activist. Like an adolescent full of urgency and outrage, you may at times get frustrated, and wish to change the world by force. But unless we approach the whole planetary system — human and natural — with gentleness and respect, we simply add to the turmoil. Easy does it. It helps to remember that the scale of things is an illusion. You can do something big, and have no effect at all, or worse, have a negative effect. You can do something small, and make all the difference. There is a need to trust, and so make our individual efforts for change in a relaxed and flexible way. We don't know how or when the kind of world we want will begin to emerge, but you can feel it coming.

One Last Story

All sanity, and all wisdom, depend on us keeping a sense of perspective.

We live in a universe which, as far as we can tell, is a place mostly of fire and dust and vast empty space. On a few moist, green specks amidst a desert of stars, it has brought forth life. The life itself swirls and recombines in exquisite complexity and richness. There is more variety in the tip of your finger, or the petal of a flower, than in the next million light years of emptiness.

Sometimes we stumble so blindly along, we never notice how precious or unique life really is, until it is gone. The bereavement columns of newspapers are full of pathetic regret — things that would have been better expressed in the midst of life. People take the miraculous for granted, until it suddenly ends.

The opposite can occur too, especially to parents of young children. We are sometimes so aware of our children's apparent vulnerability, their specialness in our hearts, that we freeze up on the joy of their simply being alive right now.

This final story is our own. A sudden series of events resulted in a fusion of commitment and emotion more intense than we had known was possible. It was as if we learned to appreciate the moment, and relax about the future, all at once. Many parents reading this will have made this jump of understanding, and will know what we mean . . .

It's about four o'clock on a wintery Sunday afternoon. Some friends have just left, and our nine-week-old baby son is having a nap in the bedroom. He's been asleep for perhaps half-an-hour, perhaps three-quarters (you don't take much notice of these things until later, looking back). Shaaron goes in to check if the baby is okay. In seconds I hear her scream my name out loud. At that point everything changes.

One's mind works so fast sometimes – already I don't want to know. I don't want to go in there, but I do. Shaaron is pulling and kneading at baby Rohan, his face is blue and still, the pupils of his little eyes rolled back alarmingly. We start yelling at him 'Breathe Rohan! Breathe!'. Shaaron starts mouth-to-mouth, and I think, 'well, she's a nurse. She'll fix things', but I'm far from sure. I run to the phone in the next room, and start dialling 000. My hand (and in fact my whole body) is shaking so much that it takes me three tries to get it right. I force myself to steady down, and finally I get through. The operator is efficient, she takes me seriously, and the ambulance people answer in seconds. They are clear, calm, and fast. They are on their way.

Shaaron says 'He's got a heartbeat. I think it's still beating'. I can't bear to look her in the eye. We take turns to blow air into Rohan, covering his tiny face and nose easily with our mouths. He feels cold. I remember to blow gently, not to injure his little lungs. We watch desperately for some sign of recovery, but there's nothing there. The eyes are still rolled back and his little body is soggy and loose, unfamiliar. I feel it's not really him. We are yelling all the time 'We want you! We love you! Stay alive Rohan!'. This does not seem crazy, either then, or now looking back.

We use a cold washcloth on his body to shock him awake. He stirs a little, perhaps. It's hard to tell. We keep on breathing into him. He is not dead, neither is he fully alive, and it becomes a kind of holding operation, waiting for the ambulance. Then it arrives. Oxygen helps, some of the blueness goes away. I'm a little embarrassed with strangers in my house, then forget it. A second ambulance team comes, they are (we guess and confirm later) the 'dead baby team'. They help out a little, then leave. We carry Rohan amidst oxygen hoses and batterypacks into the normal, green rainy street. Are our neighbours watching? How could they not, our front lawn looks like a movie set. We travel in the ambulance slowly along familiar roads that are now, forever, changed. Everything important to me is inside that van. Nothing outside matters, it is a dream.

It's not over yet. At the hospital I notice the ambulancemen tense up, they seem already angry with the nurses in casualty before they start to talk. I've heard about this problem. A nurse asks what has happened and they won't tell her. 'Get the resident. We don't want to go through this all three times over.' Something like that. For some reason I am getting angry too, on top of all the fear. We have a live baby, pink and breathing now, but still very dazed and unnaturally sleepy. But why has all this happened? We are in a booth with a curtain. People with injuries and nurses are walking about, people come in and go out and a young man, a resident, comes in. 'What happened?' We tell him and he goes away! Then he comes back. 'The child seems to be all right now. You should be right to go home now.' Doesn't he know how such imprecision hurts? We don't want to go home, we want to know what has happened and why? Is there damage? What if it happens again? We insist on staying in the hospital.

Casual, chatting people in the reception office keep me waiting. It's just another day for them. There are ten long minutes of filling in forms, with us still in our house slippers and old tracksuits, clutching our baby in an ambulance blanket. I am dazed and feel angry and passed around.

I'm a sea of impulses. I go back through Casualty, see the young resident at a desk. People ignore me so I interrupt him from the paperwork. I feel so idiotic beseeching this man, apologising for intruding, I know you have forms to fill in, but does my child have brain damage? Is the course of my life forever altered? I hope I don't actually say all these things. He looks at me distractedly. No, it should be fine. His flippant certainty sets my head hammering. Of course, it's a dumb question. He couldn't know. No-one could know yet. Damage is quite possible. But maybe not.

We go up to the Sick Babies ward; they need to know all over again what happened. We recount the story, they are kind and find us a room we can sleep in with Rohan. We ask for a breathing monitor in case we fall asleep. This prompts some discussion — if we are worried perhaps they should be too. They decide we'd better be on the ward, so we are moved back out of our room into a ward full of other damaged little ones, and gain some perspective on our problems.

We take turns all night to stay awake, in the corner of a ward full of sickness, baby coughs and baby groans, and a slowly turning clock, but it doesn't matter. We take turns to stay awake, listening to that most beautiful sound in the world — our baby softly breathing. Down the corridor I meet a senior nurse I know. I tell her briefly what has happened and she actually recognises and empathises with how I feel. With hardly a word her expression catches my feelings and I feel real for the first time in twelve hours. Soon after, we discharge ourselves, and go home.

We get back to our beautiful little house, and clean fresh air. We go inside and find ourselves suddenly crying floods of relief that it is over. We put on loud music and dance in celebration. Rohan is sleepy for a day or two, but soon plays again, and laughs again, and it all may never have happened. If he has lost brain cells, it doesn't show. For weeks we will not leave his side or stop listening at nighttime to check his breathing. In time, though, this need relaxes.*

We tell no-one about the event, not wanting to wrap anxiety around our child, or stay frozen by the events of a single day. The experience makes the transition in our minds from trauma, to recovery, to being grateful that it happened. (Does this sound strange to you? We have counselled dying cancer patients who had made the remarkable admission that they are grateful for cancer for it showed them how to live.) We refer to the event as Rohan's 'second birth' — an experience which made us a family. Our gratitude is for a lightning-bolt moment of totally unified effort back there in his bedroom — that we love each other, and this child, and want him to live so fiercely that he decides he will. That feeling has never left us.

One father wrote to us:

> Looking back on myself before I was a parent, I realise that although I considered my life very full, I was living in an emotionally muted way. Only when I had actually held a child of my own creating in my arms did I really know what was meant by fear, joy, anger, and the possibility of loss. No mountain climb could match the fatigue of the first twelve months of parenthood, and no applauding audience could match the pleasure of my own child running towards me with arms open wide.

Having a family meets so many primary needs. We all need daily physical touching, with familiarity and depth behind it. We need constant interaction to talk out our lives as we live them, with

---

* Some readers of this book will have lost babies through cot-death (also called Sudden Infant Death Syndrome). It is important to know that in the case above the baby still had a heartbeat, and was warm, and so resuscitation was possible. The cause of the incident is still unknown, although the infant did have a triple antigen injection two days earlier, and an unusual reaction to this has been suggested.

people who know and are invested in our words. We thrive on the energy and release of good sex, which only comes with trust and practice together. We need the security, and the freedom, which reliable relationships bring. We need the challenge of long-term commitments, of a story that is long and deep and difficult at times, but overwhelmingly worth it. Whether you are formally a partner or a parent, or neither, is insignificant. You find equivalents.

We are all parents, and we are all children, and we are all lovers. We may as well do it with style.

Good Books

We want to say that we don't read many books these days. We prefer to learn in person from good teachers and from the experiences of the people with whom we live and learn at our courses.

Nonetheless books are sometimes just what is needed, and here are some of our recommendations:

Books about families and children

Magical Child and also *Magical Child Matures* Pearce, Joseph Chilton, USA Bantam Books 1985. Good for people who love to read and think about new ideas.

Ourselves and Our Children A book by and for parents. Boston Women's Health Book Collective, NY Penguin Books 1978. A detailed resource book on the myriad aspects of parenting.

The Children on the Hill Deakin, Michael, GB Quartet Books 1972. True story of a family who devote themselves totally to educating their children at home, a controversial experiment with remarkable results.

Parenting for Peace and Justice McGinnis, Kathleen and John, NY Orbis 1981. A positive, and refreshingly non-anxious book.

Island Huxley, Aldous, Penguin Books 1962. A beautiful novel in which Huxley portrays a society where psychology and Buddhist values are given a practical form.

The Secret of Happy Children Biddulph, Steve, Sydney & London, Bay Books 1985, also USA, Stein & Day 1988. Our first book, written to give practical skills advice in a humorous, easy-to-read format.

Books about conflict resolution

The Magic of Conflict Crum, Thomas, NY Simon & Schuster 1987. A beautifully hopeful compilation of strategies and ways to look at conflict as a positive force, if you handle it right.

Toughlove York, Phyllis & David, PO Box 70 Sellersville PA 18960 USA. A short, readable handbook for getting tough with kids who are starting to get into serious trouble — drugs, the law, and so on.

Books about self development at all stages

Women as Winners — Transactional Analysis for Personal Growth Jongeward, Dorothy, and Scott, Dru, USA Addison Wesley 1976. How to figure out your past, and the way that it has set patterns for your life, which you may or (more likely) may not want to follow.

Don't Push the River Stevens, Barry, Utah Real People Press 1970. The inside story of a strong and intriguing woman.

A Good Age Comfort, Alex, Aust. Macmillan 1977. A book designed to challenge the old, and the not yet old, into revising their assumptions about this climactic stage of life. Ringingly affirms the pleasure, accomplishment, fulfilment available to those who refuse to fit the stereotypes of aging.

Working it Through Kubler Ross, Elisabeth and Warshaw, Mal, NY Macmillan 1982. The next best thing to being there — a photographic and prose account of a healing workshop for terminally ill people, those suffering loss of children and others.

Books about sex and romance

Woman's Experience of Sex Kitzinger, Sheila, GB Penguin 1983. Looks at sexuality right through a woman's life.

Private Lives Arndt, Bettina, Aust. Penguin 1986. Readable and honest book in which the author compares her own experiences, and counterpoints these with her understandings gained as Australia's best known sex therapist.

Will I like it? Mayle, Peter, London WH Allen & Co Ltd 1978. Unlike Peter Mayle's cartoon books, this book (specifically about our first ever sexual experience) is respectful of the topic, but still gentle, light and simple.

Touch Love Olivier, Sigurd, and Gorrie, Jeanette, The Amazing Aquarian Dream Factory GPO Box 4783 Sydney NSW. Remarkably touching and sensuous photographs and poetic text — a kind of pillow book — to help awaken one to the sensitivity of lovemaking.

The Lover Within Henderson, Julie, The Tiger Flower Alliance, 15 Datchett St East Balmain NSW 2401. This is a breakthrough book in the recently acknowledged area of personal energy and the connection with others.

Books to help us laugh at ourselves

How to Be Normal in Australia Treborlang, Robert, Major Mitchell Press 1987. A pretend-serious guide for foreigners in coping with Australian ways, it shows how bizarre, silly and avoidable some of our cultural norms have become.

Are you a New Rotic? Flowers, John and Schwartz, Bernard, N.J. Prentice Hall Inc 1984. A timely and hilarious send up of the overpsychologising of life!

Cassettes

Some people learn more by doing or listening than reading. We especially recommend a series of tapes which combine music, instructions, and information:

Parent Child Bonding For use in pregnancy and the early years of a child's life, to maximise early bonding or heal bonds damaged through separation at birth etc.

Creative Release For releasing old patterns of distress and promoting change and ease in reaching one's goals.

Relaxation Meditation Easily the best of the many tapes available for relaxation and clarity of mind, achieving these states in a remarkably short time.

All three tapes are available from IMPG, 42 Spensley St, Clifton Hill 3068.

Index